MASONIC HALLS
OF
SOUTH WALES

MASONIC HALLS
OF
SOUTH WALES

The Revd Neville Barker Cryer

LEWIS MASONIC
IAN ALLAN GROUP

In the same series

© 1990
N. B. Cryer

Published by Lewis Masonic
IAN ALLAN REGALIA LTD, Terminal House, Shepperton TW17 8AS
who are members of the
IAN ALLAN GROUP OF COMPANIES

First published in England in 1990

British Library Cataloguing in Publication Data
Cryer, Neville B.
  Masonic Halls of South Wales
  1. Wales. Freemasons. Lodges. Halls
  I. Title
  366.109429

ISBN 0 85318 180 2

Printed by Ian Allan Printing at their works at Coombelands in Runnymede,
England.

CONTENTS

FOREWORD

by

The Rt Hon LORD SWANSEA, D.L.

Provincial Grand Master
South Wales, Eastern Division

Brother Neville Cryer has done it again, and has produced a most fascinating and interesting account of the Masonic Halls of South Wales. This part of the country contains the homes of many ancient Lodges; and though I cannot claim to be familiar with the Halls described in Provinces other than my own, this book has whetted my appetite for further exploration.

Many Brethren probably go in and out of their local Hall with little more than a passing glance, but Bro Cryer approaches each Hall with enthusiasm and with an eye for detail that will astonish many who think they know their own Hall from roof to foundations.

He has done a great service to the Craft in his accounts of Masonic Halls in many parts of England and Wales, and the present book is a worthy addition to them. I commend it heartily to every student of Masonic history.

SWANSEA

RHAGAIR

gan

Y GWIR ANRHYDEDDUS ARGLWYDD ABERTAWE D.L.

MEISTR MAWREDDOG Y DALAITH
DE CYMRU, TALAITH DDWYREINIOL

Mae'r brawd Neville Cryer wedi ei gwneud hi eto, ac mae wedi cynhyrchu adroddiad hynod o ddiddorol o'r Neuaddau Saeryddol yn Ne Cymru. Mae'r rhan yma o'r wlad yn cynwys llawer o hen Gyfrinfeydd; ac er nad wyf yn wybyddus a'r Neuaddau mewn rhanbarthau eraill, mae'r llyfr wedi codi archwaeth ynof i ddarganfod mwy.

Mae'n siwr fod llawer o'r Brodyr yn mynd a dod i'w Neuaddau lleol heb sylwi ar fawr ddim, ond mae'r Brawd Cryer yn cyrraedd pob Neuadd gyda brwdfrydedd a llygad at fanylder fydd yn synnu llawer sy'n meddwl eu bod yn adnabod eu Neuadd eu hunain o'r to i'w seiliau.

Cyflawnodd wasanaeth da i'r Grefft yn ei adroddiad o'r Neuaddau Saeryddol yn llawer o ardaloedd yng Nghymru a Lloegr, ac mae'r llyfr presennol yn ychwanegiad arall teilwng iawn. Rwyn ei gymeradwyo'n frwd iawn i bob un sydd a diddordeb mewn hanes Saeryddol.

ABERTAWE

THE WRITING OF this book, like the other volumes in this series, has given the author a great deal of pleasure. It has enabled me to appreciate afresh the breadth and depth of Welsh Freemasonry and allowed me to see the wealth of treasures which we still possess from the past. It has also given me the delight of meeting some of those dedicated masons who are prepared to maintain for the future the heirlooms of buildings and contents that they have received from the past.

It has been a journey of constant surprises as door after door has been opened to reveal the temple interiors and their contents, with some of them in almost the same arrangement as that which met our forebears 150 or 100 years ago. It is the joy of that discovery, and the interest aroused in seeing so many items of peculiar fascination for the masonic student, that led me to believe that we should produce this and the other volumes.

My first concern therefore has been to record for the present generation of Welsh masons and their posterity something of what Masonry has handed down to us from its very beginnings in this land. Many, I believe, will, like myself, be pleasantly surprised by the variety and richness of the different halls which are featured here and the companion volume, *Masonic Halls of North Wales*, whether it be the Victorian grandeur of Cardiff or the modest intimacy of Denbigh, the Regency richness of Newport or the blend of old and new at Mold. Every location has its own fascination especially when, as I hope I have shown, the building also contains special treasures that are known nowhere else or only rarely so. I hope that this survey of Welsh Halls will raise the spirits of masons in the Principality and make them freshly proud of the heritage that is theirs.

The second purpose of my writing has been to try and encourage a greater diligence in looking at and understanding the possessions in Freemasonry that we may have in our own locality. It has been my experience that my visit to a temple or the museum attached to it has often renewed interest in its contents for the masons who regularly and normally meet there. Too many of us are not aware of the treasure trove that lies around us and there is all the more danger that if this unconscious indifference is not stemmed there could be examples of the kind of loss of previous pieces of the past such as have already occurred in some centres. If you ask some masons in a place that already has a long tradition where are their old tracing boards, banners, pillars or pottery the answer is either 'we never did know what happened to them' or 'Ah! now we do have something like that stacked away somewhere'. Readers of this book will discover that one hall lost its oldest banners because a heating engineer threw them out as 'unwanted rubbish' and another had its oldest banner and first Victorian candidate's clothing in a trunk in a side 'junk room'. I would hope that others might, like them, avoid unnecessary loss and retrieve what is a link with a proud past.

Thirdly, I want to encourage masons who travel round the Principality to go and see some of the halls and their contents that are mentioned here. It has long been a custom for tourists to seek out old parish churches, castles or manor houses and the setting up of 'CADW' in Wales rightly encourages such a sense of appreciating and learning from the past. Here, for Freemasons, is the beginning of a guide for those who wish to look at our peculiar heritage from the past of Wales. I even hope that readers will take this book with them on their journeys and ring up the hall, Provincial or lodge secretary and ask whether a visit to these halls is possible. It will well repay you to see these halls for yourself.

As I have travelled around a good deal of Wales and responded to the information regarding interesting halls that has been provided for me I have been only too well aware that I may be overlooking some gem of masonic interest that I ought to have included here. Despite my attempt to be thorough I am sure that there will be someone who will want to draw my attention to a treasure overlooked. With the encouragement of the publisher I invite anyone who would wish to do so to write to me at Shepperton and give me details of what it is they think that I should see. I am sure that if there were a future edition of this work it would only benefit by being fully comprehensive. What such contacts would do would be to ensure that this book had already begun to make more masons aware of and concerned about the *Masonic Halls of Wales*.

The Revd Neville Barker Cryer
1990

NO BOOK SUCH as this could possibly have been completed without the help of a large number of collaborators. I shall attempt to name many of these below but it would be impossible to mention the countless Provincial Grand Masters, Provincial Grand Secretaries and their staffs, who have assisted me with suggestions, contacts, directions for travel, and in some cases actual hospitality. I am deeply grateful to them all and I want to state here that had it not been for them and their work then this book would not have been possible and certainly not in the time span that it has taken.

Having been put in touch with individual halls and the lodges associated with them I especially want to thank the following for their interest before, during and following my visits and for being willing in each case to check the script of my chapters for their hall so that it is as accurate as possible. Any remaining errors must be laid at my door.

(Abergavenny) J. Straker and D. A. Thomas; (Carmarthen) G. Lodwick; (Cardiff) K. Flynn and E. Haydn Lloyd; (Cardigan) K. May and B. V. Rees; (Fishguard) Dr P. J. Croxford, T. M. Evans and R. Warburton; (Haverford-west) J. Young; (Llanelli) W. S. Thomas; (Merthyr Tydfil) H. L. Collins and M. Williams; (Milford Haven) A. Corey; (Monmouth) L. E. Hayward; (Neath) M. C. Fish and G. L. Rowlands; (Newport) G. Carey, P. R. Redpath and G. Vernon; (Pembroke Dock) H. Harries; (Swansea) G. Challenger, R. Harris, M. J. Hoare, and C. Lewis, G. Pattinson and H. F. Thomas, (Neyland) A. T. G. Cummings; (Narberth) M. Lewis and J. A. Waddia; (Chepstow) D. Powell.

I must pay a special tribute here to Lawrie C. Stokes of Lamphey near Pembroke who not only acted as host and driver for many visits but helped to coordinate the work in South West Wales and has been a very good friend and colleague. Numerous photographers, most of them professional artists, have supplied the illustrations but some of those who provided pictures were so generous as to make them gifts and they should be mentioned: Anton Attard Photography (Cardiff) Haydn Jones (Swansea and Neath), and David Llewelyn (Llanelli).

To all these brethren, as well as many others whom I have met and may not have mentioned, I extend the very warmest of thanks for all their help and express my delight at having made so many more Welsh masonic friends.

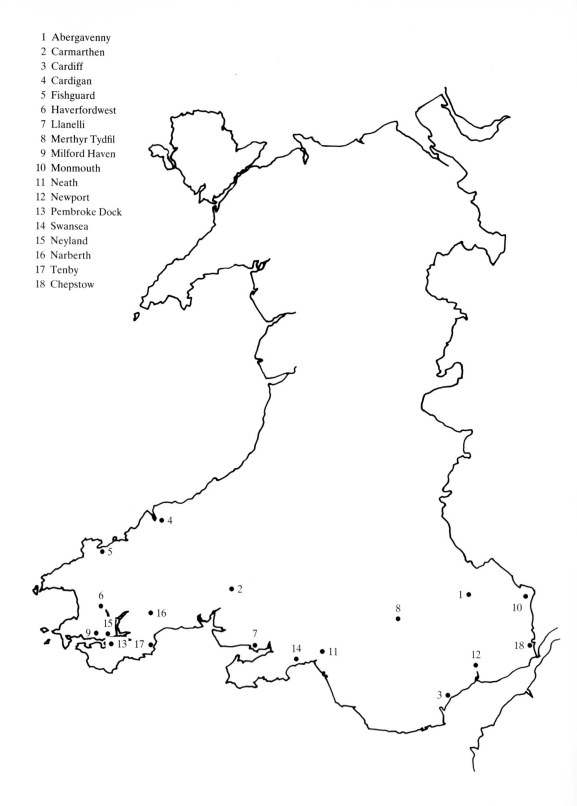

ABERGAVENNY

(Y FENNI)

Parish Church and Masonic Hall

FINDING MASONIC HALLS is sometimes far from easy and you could have great difficulty in discovering the one in Abergavenny. You need to walk down to where the main street of the town has become a pedestrian precinct and start looking for a narrow lane that leads off it called St John's Street. Go down here twenty yards and you will come to a high wall with a double gate marked by a large arch. Above the wall upon will see what looks like, and once was, a lofty church tower made of local sandstone. Beside the gate is a blue plaque which marks this as a place of local historic interest. It reads: 'King Henry VIII Grammar School 1543-1898'. You have arrived at what for Abergavenny masons is home.

The antiquity of their meeting place was well described by WBro I. T. Williams when this hall was dedicated for its present purpose in November 1899. He stated that 'it was practically admitted that this was the ancient parish church of Abergavenny, known as St John's, and it was founded at an exceedingly early period. Its great antiquity has been established in a variety of ways. For instance, the altar stone, discovered a few years ago and concealed over the fireplace in an adjoining house, is supposed to have been in use about the year AD 1100, and it is thought by many competent to judge that it was in use at a far earlier period than that. It has since been presented to Holy Trinity Church, where it is now used for its original purpose. The west doorway, which still exists, is probably of the Early Decorated period of 1420. During the recent alterations an early English piscina of about the 13th century was unearthed in the east wall of the north transept. This was also presented to Holy Trinity Church. No evidence can be found showing how the church of St Mary became the parish church and the church of St John came to be used as the Grammar School. It is, however, an undisputed fact that Henry VIII both disestablished and disendowed the Priory and established the Grammar School, endowing it with part of the (priory) funds. To possess as we do, an ancient embattled tower is unique in the history of Masonic Temples.' (*Freemasonry in Monmouthshire*, p120) When he first spoke those words Bro Williams was probably correct. Today the masons of Guy's Cliffe in Warwickshire would want to contend this claim to uniqueness. (See *Masonic Halls of England — The Midlands*.)

The school that was here in Tudor times continued to be held in this same building until some time between 1898 and the following year. The Governors had by then built a new school in response to the needs of a growing population, and the old church of St John had already been sold to a gentleman who in turn had transferred the possession of it to the local freemasons. It is for this reason that an extract from the minutes of the lodge in Abergavenny for 1895 (21 October) states that the building had been purchased by a sub-committee of the lodge for the sum of £800.

The 'building' thus referred to was a nave with a tower at the east end, a pointed window and door at the west end and other windows at the sides. This present tower is not the one so referred to but is only about 200 years old. The

Left: The old church tower now part of the masonic hall in Abergavenny. The tower is 18th century although part of the building is 15th century.

15

walls of the church are much older though other buildings were from time to time allowed to be erected alongside these from time to time. It cannot therefore be claimed that all the walls of the present temple are of the same ancient stonework. What can be claimed and proudly maintained is that masons of St John's Lodge, No 818, still assemble on a site of 'time immemorial' sanctity. It is a hall that befits as well as reflects their ancestry.

The actual name of St John was not assumed until the time that its members took up residence in this property. Prior to that time, and from the year 1860 when today's lodge was first constituted, the lodge was called 'Philanthropic' and it met first at the Angel Hotel, in Cross Street. The lodge next met in what had been the previous Catholic chapel of the town which certainly seemed a fitting prelude to the eventual move to old St John's, and this was followed by some 33 years in the Masonic Hall off Lion Street. What seems to have been a continuing lodge and 'church' connection was also evident in 1872 when Provincial Grand Lodge met under the Philanthropic banner on 20 June. The brethren formed a procession and marched to Trinity Church, headed by the band of the 94th Regiment, and there listened to a very eloquent sermon preached by Bro the Rev W. D. Horwood. The collection, be it noted, was given to an 'outside cause', the funds of the local Dispensary.

Yet this Philanthropic Lodge was not itself the first such lodge in Abergavenny. A petition had been granted in December 1814 for a Philanthropic Lodge No 648 to meet at the King's Head Inn which still stands at one end of the High Street. This lodge too had 'church' connections for whilst one clergyman, the Rev James Ashby Gabb, was nominated its first Master, it was the Rev William Powell who was in fact so installed. Seven of the ten founders were members of the Loyal Cambrian Lodge (see Merthyr Tydfil) and these included a Tudor and a schoolmaster who would have been even more overjoyed to have seen where their masonic successors were eventually to reside. It was this lodge that moved after four years to the 'Angel Inn' though that does not seem to have brought new life to the membership and in 1822 it was dormant and by 1828 removed from the Grand Lodge Roll. Short-lived it may have been but its influence and its memory were obviously such that when another Philanthropic Lodge was being formed both the name and the location were first of all those taken from the earlier ancestor.

As we shall see there are furnishings and artefacts in the present hall that speak eloquently of the two lodges that came into existence in the 19th century. What is even more striking as you visit this centre are the well preserved evidences of an even earlier gathering of masons in Abergavenny — those who were in fact French prisoners of war but lodged in this, as in certain other Welsh towns, as did many other groups in both English and Scottish locations. Before we come to that part of the story and the examples of it that can still be seen here it will be as well if we retrace our steps to the entrance gate with its attendant blue plaque.

Behind the encircling wall is a small courtyard with the tower's stonework immediately in front of us and a blue double doorway in its centre at the foot. Over the door panels with their black ornamental hinges is a semicircular fanlight of opaque white glass bearing the words 'MASONIC HALL' and these are also surrounded by another band of ornamental painted lights. The whole headpiece is completed with a band of rough ashlars that carry a hanging lamp at their apex. This is a later door to the tower for about a foot above this entrance one can very clearly pick out another string of arched stones with a very definite

Looking west with the pipe organ built into the wall. The table in the centre holds the tracing boards and has raised script on its surface.

keystone at its head. This was probably the original East window of the structure behind though the outer limits of any such window have been lost in the repair work that has obviously been done from time to time. Above a second string course we see a modern lancet window in the face of the tower and two more appear at regular intervals above in stages. One suspects that these gave light to additional, later classrooms that were created in this way.

To the right of the tower as we approach it there is a much more modern two-storeyed pebbledashed house with a small but inscribed brass plaque on the upper part of its black front door. The wording reads:

'This Tyler's Residence was opened by WBro the Hon Sir Walter Vaughan Morgan, Bart. PGW, PGT, Lord Mayor of London, on 8 September 1906.'

This house is balanced by another dwelling on the left of the tower save that whilst the Tyler's house is at right angles to the tower this two storeyed structure built in 1760 is like an addition to the lower tower and proves the point made earlier that further rooms were joined on to the original church walls. Into the lower floor of this 'house' we shall shortly pass. It too was obviously a classroom or staff room previously but is now known as the Committee room though it was once the dining room when the number of members was more modest. To reach it we enter the tower doorway and find ourselves in the rather spartan vestibule, with a flight of enclosed stairs rising above us to the right. It is here that we make our first 'discovery' that takes us back to the earliest days of known Freemasonry in this town.

Opposite the entrance and hung on the walls that flank a further doorway we see two unusual carved objects. They are made from oak and the exact meaning of them has never been fully discovered, though examination of them does begin to offer some clues. What seems certain is that they were intended by the French masons who first possessed or made them to be placed, as here, at or near the entrance of their lodge room. Their design is neo-classical, which suggests an 18th century derivation, and though the three panels which are in their setting were once coloured but have now been almost obliterated, one might guess at what they portrayed.

The elongated lower panel stands at the end of a narrow chamber which is designed as in perspective with a chequered flooring and tapering walls with domed ceiling. Here might well be displayed one of the saints John before the red and blue curtains of the Holy of Holies which was at the end of the vault. The two pillars flanking the whole lower part of the object suggest an entrance to the Temple. Next, between the heavy chapiters, is a second panel beneath the cornice and this might well have displayed the sun, moon and stars. Whilst at the top of the item between the separated, curved branches of the headpiece there is what looks for all the world like an altar or pedestal on the front of which there was probably a scene connected with some part of the ritual. Traces of colour are still clear and the two portable objects may well have been rich adornments of the French lodge here. They are certainly unique as furnishings of a British lodge and further information about them from any reader will be welcome.

It is when we pass through the door of the room to the left of this vestibule that we are again reminded of the French connection. Facing the visitor as he enters are four well-kept and framed certificates which will inevitably draw the immediate attention of any masonic student. Before we examine them in more detail, however, it will be as well to provide a little background for those to whom the whole story of the French prisoner-of-war lodges in England is unfamiliar. For those wanting to study the matter in full reference should be made to the book by John T. Thorp published in and after 1900.

From 1740 to 1815 Great Britain and France were in almost constant conflict with one another. As a result a large number of prisoners fell into the hands of British commanders who shipped them to this island where some of them were to reside for lengthy periods of time. In 1759 there were 11,000 men in one location alone — at Knowle, near Bristol — but by far the greatest number were sent during the Revolutionary period from 1797 to 1814. Of 122,000 French soldiers and sailors who were despatched here after 1803 and the Peninsular War campaign, 17,000 were exchanged for Englishmen who were prisoners in France of corresponding rank, many were invalided home, 10,000 died in captivity and several hundreds of commissioned officers broke parole and escaped from the country. In the last year of this period however 67,000 men were still being held and were returned home when peace was signed.

The common soldiers and sailors were mostly confined in huge barracks or prisons and the gaol at present on Dartmoor was one of those specially erected for this purpose. Some were kept on board 'prison hulks' or discarded ships as at Chatham and Portsmouth. The officers, and those civilians entitled to rank as 'gentlemen', were allowed to reside 'on parole' within assigned limits and on certain conditions. They were usually placed in smaller provincial towns and, writes Thorp, 'being in many cases men of rank and education, were esteemed for their polite and agreeable manners, and were received in all public assemblies with high consideration and courteous welcome.' In Wales such places were chosen as Chepstow, Caernarfon, Pembroke and of course Abergavenny. Whilst their general conditions of detention were made as little irksome as possible the mere fact of being under restraint was galling for many of this proud race. One further embarrassing factor for this latter group of Frenchman must have been the fact that it appears that the French government never contibuted one penny to the maintenance of this host of captives whereas the English authorities regularly remitted large sums for the upkeep of English troops in prison abroad.

Since Freemasonry was as popular in the French, as it was in the British, army at this period it was hardly surprising that amongst the thousands of French officers and men who thus came to live in England, Scotland and Wales there were a great number of masons. What is more we know that the English Craft took numerous steps to alleviate the distress of these French brethren, as old lodge minute books frequently record. We even have one occasion when the Grand Lodge itself voted a substantial amount to assist a naval commander who was 'on parole' in Launceston, Cornwall. There was also one officer of high rank who spent his captivity as the guest of the Duke of Devonshire and who, on his return after the war, declared that his stay there had been 'the happiest period of his life thus far'.

Where local lodges were already in existence these French-prisoner brethren were often welcomed as visitors or became joining members, but where, as in Abergavenny, there was no lodge in existence and the French had enough of their number to open and work a lodge themselves, they appear to have done so. In Abergavenny such seems to have been the case with French masons establishing the first traces of the organised Craft in this place. What is even more to the point is that whilst these lodges were probably held without any warrant or authority whatever and were confined normally to the French brethren who held them, there is clear evidence that in some cases they initiated, and in others accepted as joining members, local Welshmen or Englishmen who lived where these prisoner-of-war meetings were held.

With upwards of 200 prisoners located at Abergavenny it is not surprising that a lodge was formed in this town by at least 1813. Considering that the first members were French soldiers and sailors the name chosen for their lodge was highly appropriate — 'Enfants de Mars et de Neptune'. Tradition has it that they met in a large room in Monk Street, fittingly one hundred yards from the Old Priory Church of St Mary, and in which the officers locally held their mess room. A picture of this room, with its arched roof and heavily moulded ceiling, is still extant but though it was for long a solicitor's office in the 19th century it was finally closed in 1909 and pulled down with the surrounding property. The four certificates that hang today upon the walls of the Abergavenny Masonic Hall were issued to the members of this French Lodge in a 'foreign' town and any visitor here will do well to observe the lay-out, decoration and seals on these documents for they are indeed a real part of the masonic traditions of this place.

Interestingly the earliest of these certificates is to an Englishman, Benjamin Plummer, whilst two others were to Thomas Richards, a local merchant and native of the town. Both of these brethren were 'joining members'. The Plummer certificate is a parchment document (16in by 14in) which is a copy of the ordinary engraved French types of the period. Its content is very similar to that of Richard's but it is inferior in richness of symbols and in the execution of the script. It was of course the case that French certificates at this period were more varied in design than those issued by the premier Grand Lodge of England but yet there were certain common characteristics that usually appeared and are seen here. These are a cloudy canopy at the head, with representations of the sun, moon and seven stars flanking an irradiated triangle. On either side of the certificate is a lofty pillar bearing either J or B. Stretching over the whole head of the document is a thrice-looped cord with the end tassels hanging down outside the pillars. At the foot, ascended by three, five and seven steps, is a platform of squares or chequers upon which are displayed the working tools and other emblems. The figures of Minerva, Justice and Truth are frequently represented as are also Faith, Hope and Charity.

Whilst we cannot pursue all the contents of these four certificates in detail here there are five items in the Plummer certificate which help us to conjure up a

Looking east with the pillars of green marble dominant. Note the All Seeing Eye high on the east wall.

little more of the background against which this earliest practice of Freemasonry in Abergavenny took place. These details are:

(i) The lodge is dedicated to St John 'of Scotland' and held under the sanction of the Grand Orient of France.

(ii) Plummer is named as 'superintendant(sic) grand commander of the order of Knights Templars &c for the principality of Wales' under the patronage of the Duke of Kent;

(iii) Plummer is further described as 'past senior grand Warden of the free and accepted masons *in* England, according to the old Constitution (his grace the Duke of Athold)' (sic);

(iv) Born in Somerset Plummer was yet a commercial agent resident in London who also had been a member of the French lodge of 'Desired Peace' at Wimcanton(sic) in Somerset;

(v) The certificate is signed by the 'Venerable en exercice' (Acting Wor Master) De Grasse-Tilly,33°: S.W. E.Deprinche,R. . C.; J.W. Ormier du Medie, K. . H. . 30° amongst many other Rose Croix masons, whilst the whole is sealed and stamped by the Guardian of seals, G.Laudy, who gives the number 26 to this brother's certificate.

A picture that emerges from the above items is of a lodge of Frenchmen, using their own language, who have already admitted 25 other persons into their company by the time that Bro Plummer comes on the scene. Albeit a London mason, having been initiated in the Royal Athelstan Lodge in 1798, Bro Plummer not only knows that there is a French lodge in his native county but is accepted into it and then finds the French lodge three counties away across the Severn estuary. That he could know this because he was also Commander of the Knights Templar in Wales seems clear especially as some of these Frenchmen would be associated with that order which, as in the Camp of Baldwyn at Bristol to this day (and Plummer was a member there also), the Knights Templar and Rose Croix degrees were very closely allied. Nor was this all. Not only was Plummer an Antients mason who would naturally think of other orders being connected with a Craft lodge but he was also a commercial agent or dealer in masonic clothing and equipment. This is shown by a minute in the first Philanthropic Lodge book for 1815 where we are told that they paid a bill for belts due to Plummer. Belts for a lodge that probably still used swords as in Bristol degree working today is a natural purchase but one suspects that he also sold such items to the French Rose Croix masons earlier since they certainly needed them. One forebears to suggest that business benefit led to Plummer's memberships but it cannot have done him any harm.

It is finally to be remarked from this certificate that the Grand Orient of France, which today is regarded as irregular by British standards because it does not require belief in the GAOTU, is here shown as having a dedication to a Christian Saint, albeit not one of the usual Saints John. Of course the fact that one of the signatories was De Grasse Tilly, Sovereign Grand Commander of the Ancient and Accepted Scottish Rite, might well account for the Saint's orientation. It is quite a thought that one whose office in England and Wales today would be highly regarded was yet another prisoner of war in this lodge and town. Moreover, we need to note that in the office of Seals Keeper we have Gaspard Laudy who is the recipient of one of these four certificates, only this time, like the second one of Thomas Richards's, it is a certificate for the Rose Croix chapter associated with the lodge. Two phrases of the latter certificates is here worth recording but this is not the place for comment upon their fuller significance:

'We . . . summoned and assembled in a place Wherein reign Faith, Hope and Charity; seeing the Zeal and eagerness that our most Dear and Perfect Brother . . . has to attain the degree and perfect point of masonry . . . do hereby unanimously declare our M. . D. . B. . Thomas Ricard (sic) to be a member of our S. in Chapter . . .

'. . . under the Title of R. . +. . of Heredon that he may enjoy all the prerogatives attached to that respectable degree . . .'

Moreover the certificates are sealed with red wax pendant from six narrow ribbons of white, light blue, black, scarlet, dark green and crimson. Those colours alone are worth a study.

If one turns about after studying these ancient and intriguing documents and looks at the wall in which the door stands one sees yet another link with this early period of Abergavenny Masonry. Here are two large glass cases displaying officers' collars of an unusual design since the two flat ends of the material hanging from the neck are joined by a triangular piece with its point downwards.

A decorated door light inside the old church.

These collars are exactly the same as those found in the hall of Loyal Cambrian Lodge at Merthyr Tydfil and this is hardly surprising since it was brethren from this latter lodge who helped to form the lodge that followed on from the French one. Was it perhaps the consecrating officer of the first Philanthropic Lodge, Benjamin Plummer no less, who was the supplier for both centres? Today, after the newly agreed form of collars was accepted in the later 19th century, these items remain as the link with the past.

Indeed, says Thorp in his account, 'At the conclusion of peace in May 1814, the French prisoners were at liberty to return home, of which privilege no doubt the majority availed themselves. The English members of the Lodge, eleven in number, immediately formed themselves into a Lodge of Instruction to meet weekly at the King's Head Inn, until, as their minutes of 22 July 1814, state, a dispensation or a Dormant Warrant could be procured.' The subsequent development we have already described. What we have not yet said is that the Rev William Powell, the Vicar of Abergavenny, the first Master of the new lodge, was known to have been a sincere friend to the French prisoners who often referred to the many acts of kindness and consideration which he had displayed towards them. It is also worth recording that down to 1860 there were still two brethren living in Abergavenny who claimed to have been initiated in the French Prisoners lodge, whether that was regular or not.

It was not just the old collars worn by members of three successive lodges in Abergavenny that helped to create a sense of continuity in this place. When the present premises were opened for masonic use in 1899 J. H. Taylor, PPGW (South Wales Eastern Division) presented to the then Worshipful Master a curious snuff box which he had acquired from a friend who had recently paid a visit to France. Beautifully carved out of a marrow bone by a French freemason who was confined as a prisoner of war in the town of Abergavenny, Taylor desired to present it to that lodge which was the descendant, in one sense, of that period. The gift was most gratefully received and is a treasured possession of the present hall. Once again the links over 175 years have been retained.

Besides these distinctive items there are others in the 'committee room'. There are two charming brass coffee pots, two further certificates in French by the window looking into the courtyard, and in between the cases with the old collars another framed item showing the style of old tracing boards that are still extant in Merthyr Tydfil and some of the older jewels used in this building. Of these all remain except the very ornate Master's jewel which must surely be pre-Union. Between the legs of a compass extended on a segment of a circle below there is in descending order an open book, a radiant sun with a face, two pillars with a shovel, level and pick between and the whole in silver gilt. The two wardens' jewels also show that besides having an inscribed pillar on their central space they were also intended originally to have brilliants in their bases (see Carmarthen). Moreover the elegant bureau with its solid doors above, given by H. P. Cadle, a grocer in the town, further conveys the sense of dignity and richness to this outer room. One might well wonder if there could be anything more to see, especially as the walls here have provided so much of interest already. There is indeed more to come, though both of the items are rather hidden away.

The first is at the back of the mantelpiece in this room and perhaps easily overlooked by the visitor. It is a delicate miniature portrait painted by another French prisoner of war and showing an unknown brother. As one considers it one is as captivated by its attention to detail as one is by those other, more frequently encountered, miniature tracing boards under glass that these prisoner artists found time to create. Here again we are transported back in time to that

A dome for use in Royal Arch ceremonies complete with removable stones.

earlier age and aware that such are this hall's collection of treasures that this mere item can be almost left aside.

The other item is far from small but it is hidden from view under the large table that occupies most of the centre of the committee room. It is the original tracing board container made for the second Philanthropic Lodge and whilst its dimensions and design in general are no different from many others around the country the fact that it is creamy white and has a top surface entirely covered in raised blue lettering with a gold decoration around its sides must make it one of the most unusual holders of its kind. The wording is worth recording:

'Thus saith the Lord God. Behold I lay in Zion for a foundation a stone a tried stone a precious corner stone a sure foundation. He that believeth shall not make haste to judgement. Also evil I lay to the line and righteousness to the plummet.'

When laid in the centre of the temple that we shall shortly visit this box must be a feature of no little attention, as well as being far from easy to manoeuvre. There must be many who come to this hall and never see this peculiarly striking and spiritual piece of furniture.

Yet it is time now to retrace our steps and return to the vestibule. Turning left we pass through a bright blue door with a stained glass fanlight containing a silver square and compasses on a dark blue roundel surrounded by a formal decorative design of orange, green and black, and enter the anteroom which stretches across the whole width of the old church. Facing us is a small lodge library on open shelves, a picture above of a Bro Gardner whose family served as tylers in this hall for over 100 consecutive years whilst to the left of this area we see another light blue door over the lintel of which is another portion of Victorian stained glass. This comes from the old Raven Inn which then became a grocer's shop for a time. As such it was the home of H. P. Cadle, a Philanthropic/St John's member, who handed over this fragment of glass to the lodge members. Once again we have that sense of local pride and continuity which is so strong in this building and there will be other examples of a like kind when we look around the temple to which this door now leads us.

Such is the antiquity of the structure that now surrounds us that though in fact brethren have met here for only the last 90 years one has a sense of going back to at least the start of the French lodge's activities. This is almost certainly due to the general decor, the dark barrel roof and ceiling, the heavy canopy-style draperies that fall from the tooth-ornamented white cornice in the east and south, the huge expanses of light blue walling with an arch of it in the east above the Master, and in that arch a single All-seeing Eye. One is also aware of the well-filled brown Past Masters' boards in the south and the rows of plain but red-covered benches that stand out against the lower plain white walls, the framed portraits on the south wall, the solid but straightforward, round-backed Victorian upright chairs, and the no less solid mantelpiece behind the Secretary's knee-hole desk. The original fireplace is now filled with a plain white surround and a dark and light blue chequered tiling at its centre. One has the real sense of being in a long-standing family meeting place with its chequered carpeting over the whole floor.

What is more unusual in this temple is the preponderance of white among the lodge furniture. As we have seen there is a white and blue tracing board box that graces the lodge floor, the pedestals of the principal officers are also white, and tapered, and the bases of the two pillars in the west are also cubes of white. This, together with the panelling mentioned earlier, relieves what might otherwise be a very sombre room and it must have been the impression that the first members of a Philanthropic lodge wanted to convey for the furniture dates from Regency rather than from Victorian times. The pillars in the west of the floor area are striking because above their white cubes they have gold bases, dark green marbled columns and gold chapiters, with fine globes in their frames on the top. In many a larger room, as at Llanelli, it may well have been thought that these pillars were nowadays an impediment to movement but here they remain and bring distinction and continuity to an ancient lodge room.

Whilst in the west our attention may be peculiarly drawn to certain items which further distinguish this temple from any others. Most of the west wall behind the Senior Warden's place is occupied by a very fine pipe organ which has a built-in console and to its right, as you look down the temple, is the inner side of the entrance door. This has the appearance of an arched gateway with a most definite keystone at its apex. Yet it is on the left of the organ that our attention is most likely to be fixed for here we find a heavy, carved wooden bar across the corner of the blue-walled room and hanging from the bar a large church bell. This used to be in the church tower of this building and was used to sound the 'Curfew' in past days. The oak beam that bears it is covered with various items such as a heavy maul, a skull and crossbones, a level and plumb, and at its centre the words:

'This bell was placed in its present position by WBro W. D. Steel, during his year of office, 1904-5'.

This bell is still used during certain ceremonial work and its place here seems fitting for part of the town's and lodge's past.

Below this beam and bell stands a most intriguing dome. It is, one discovers, light enough to move and when placed in the body of the lodge room, as it usually is for Chapter work, one sees that it has three removable cope stones at the top of the dome and what is meant to be broken masonry at one side. Its purpose for those familiar with the Royal Arch Chapter will be at once clear but it must be one of the very few such items in England or Wales, even though arches are common in many other parts. It certainly gives the impression of having been used for some considerable time but the date of its introduction is not known.

Turning once more to the east end of the temple we must look more carefully at the items that comprise the Master's place. In front of his white pedestal, with its gold decoration and red plush cushion for his ivory gavel, there is a lean-to open-carved desk on which the VSL is placed. The Bible is obviously original, with a tooled cover on which is a pair of opened compasses embracing a glory above a free-standing square in the centre and a sun, moon, ladder and level at the four corners. Of this volume and other items close by we read in the inventory of the first Philanthropic Lodge in 1816 which states, amongst other things, that there were:

> 'Large Crimson Canopy Chair, £9 12s 0d. Two common Harm (sic) chairs, £2. Six Candle sticks with Brass Nosles and white metal stands . . . Two Flanel Jackets and two flanel Drawers . . . Ten belts . . . Smooth and Rough Astler (ashlar), 1 Coff,Boards,1 Bible . . . 1 Woodwink (sic), 11 Swords . . .'

The large Crimson Canopy chair seems to have disappeared but one of the common 'Harm chairs' has been retained and now has an honoured place as the

A Certificate issued to Benjamin Plummer by a French prisoner of war lodge formed in Abergavenny.

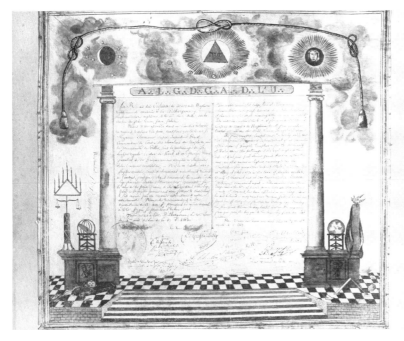

seat of the IPM. We might well regard it as a noble piece of early 19th century furniture with red brocade upholstery, an oval back panel, finely turned frame, arms and legs. Whether it was felt to be too fragile for regular use by the Master or whether the new Philanthropic Lodge wanted their own set of principal chairs, as they certainly have, one cannot know. Perhaps the IPM had already laid claim to it. Whatever the reason we see now a much more substantial Victorian chair for the officers, with light oak, strong legs and frame, two very substantial pillars framing the backpiece (with their own spheres) and the upholstery in hard-wear leather. The chair is raised on a substantial base of chequered design and behind it there hangs the earliest banner of St John's Lodge presented 120 years ago by the then Master-elect, W. Williams, junr. It is edged and embroidered with bullion lace and bears the name, number and crest of the lodge. Behind this banner there can be made out the outline of the old west door of the church.

Of the remainder of the inventory mentioned above we still see the 'nosles' of the candlesticks, even it there are no white stands (which would have matched the pedestals). The mention of 'flanel' clothing reminds the reader of this volume that such have just been found in the Royal Denbigh lodge room, 'lost' in another oddments chest, and the 'coff' here was doubtless that box for the tracing boards which we found in the committee room. The swords obviously fitted the ten belts, with one loose in the hands of the tyler, whilst the presence of only one 'hoodwink' would confirm that multiple initiations were not normal.

The only other items which we should note before we leave this fascinating temple and hall are a loving cup, usually standing on the mantelpiece behind the Secretary, and a coloured photograph in the supper room. The silver cup was used for many years at the lodge's Annual Festival when it was the custom, after the new officers had been invested, to pass this cup round (appropriately filled of course) so that those present in the temple could extend hearty good wishes to the newly installed Master. One is inevitably reminded of the custom in Ludlow's ancient Silurian Lodge where at much the same time *after* the Union of the Grand Lodges it was still the case that they brought a punch bowl into the lodge room so that the past Masters present could honour the new entrant to their ranks (See *Masonci Halls of England — The Midlands*).

The other items used to be in the old Supper Room. Amongst a collection of various interesting items — an engraving of the Scald Masons, a parchment certificate from the Union Lodge at the Cape of Good Hope in 1824 and a large Engraved Plate of the List of Lodges by B. Pickart, 1735 — there was an old Parchment Certificate (Royal Arch) issued to Samuel Cooper in 1835 and given to the Hall in 1910 by W. P. Cooper. I say that it *was* there for it now transpires that this certificate has been returned to the Royal Cumberland Chapter in Bath where it will have a fine home in the museum there (see *Masonic Halls of England — The South*).

As we leave the Supper Room, pass through the vestibule and cross the courtyard on our way into the outside world once more one cannot but rejoice to have found so much of interest, besides the fact that any passer-by could cull from the white-ringed blue plaque that is affixed by the gate. Looking back at the triangle above the gate itself, beneath an arch of stone and with a circle of gold at its centre and a point within it one can only reflect that any mason who gains admittance here can hardly go wrong. His visit to the Masonic Hall of Abergavenny will be amply worthwhile.

Right: *The curfew bell originally used in the church tower of the same building now hangs in the temple room.*

THIS BELL
WAS PLACED IN ITS
PRESENT POSITION
BY
W.B.& W.D. STEEL
DURING HIS YEAR
OF OFFICE
1904-1905

CARMARTHEN
(CAERFYRDDIN)

The Hall reflecting Welsh Masonic Origins

DISCOVERING THE ORIGINS of Freemasonry in any locality is a fascinating experience. To learn how it is that the Craft which is practised today in this place or that had its beginnings is of interest to anyone with a sense of history. For some of the centres mentioned in this volume the start of local masonry is precise and well documented but in others the story is much less clear. Of nowhere in Wales is this more true than of Carmarthen. For here we begin in the realm of Time Immemorial and the possibility that there was a lodge working in the town prior to the establishment of the Premier Grand Lodge in 1717. Here certainly we have the very first indications of speculative Freemasonry in Wales, a primacy in the Craft which was to persist into the 18th century.

Why this should be is a matter that deserves careful reflection and more attention than we can give the matter here. Does the Roman name given to the town — fort by the sea — give us a clue? Was it mariners in touch with early Masonry in Bristol, Lancashire, Scotland or even London that brought the idea of a lodge to this particular (and navigable) port? Or was it that this town was for so long the posting stage of those passing from England to West Wales — again a link with Bristol and London? The proximity of a vast and constantly tapped quarry of stone in the Prescelly Mountains or nearer seams gives ample reason for recognizing the need for operative masons whilst those seeking to learn of their ways and traditions would have had ample opportunity for doing so. Speculation as all this may be the truth is that shortly after the founding of the Grand Lodge in London there was established a Province of South Wales and the basis of that arrangement was the lodge that appears to have been already meeting in this town.

One thing is certain and that is that when you have entered the Masonic Hall at Carmarthen today you are soon made aware of a long tradition of Freemasonry in these parts. This is hardly surprising in view of what has just been said but there are many instances in other parts of the Principality, as indeed in England, of traces of the past being swept away or just plain lost by those who have come after. Recognition of the importance of our origins is happily much more vigorous and lively now than it was at earlier periods. Here in Carmarthen they have been able to retain or recover some of the evidence to establish their heritage.

The hall that we are now to visit is the second of those which have stood on this site in Spilman Street. The first was erected in 1899 but it proved too modest and quite inadequate for the steadily increasing numbers of candidates and the growth of the Chapter and Mark Lodge that also used the building. In 1911 another hall was therefore built in place of the former and the consecration of another lodge in the town, the Kensington Lodge of Installed Masters, shows the need that the new premises would meet. Caerfyrddin Lodge No 4963 was to arrive in 1927.

As it is the present building is in no way pretentious. Caught fast, it would seem, between a featureless, square set of offices made of ordinary brick, and an early Victorian, cream-plastered Guest House, the façade of the hall in two shades of blue certainly stands out but is yet dominated by its neighbours. They being each of three floors and the hall having only two one gives a sense of the hall fighting for its life and perhaps the plain and unmistakable placard of its purpose — the letters MASONIC HALL in blue on its paler background and filling the whole space between the three upper and lower casement windows — proclaims clearly why it has a right to be here.

Indeed it has such a right. The oldest lodge meeting here, St Peters, No 476, was constituted in September 1841 and met at the Ivy Bush Hotel just across the street. Not only so but freemasons who had met in Carmarthen before this date also gathered at the Ivy Bush for, as one last declaration of 'authentic' Freemasonry before the swiftly approaching masonic Union of 1813, there was constituted in Carmarthen the Antients Lodge (sic) No 158. This began its life on 15 July 1811 and was then renamed the Union Lodge No 192 when it joined in 1814 with a revived Moderns lodge, Perfect Friendship. The brethren of this

Carmarthen Masonic Hall with the effective use of Doric columns that frame the windows.

new body also met at the Ivy Bush Hotel, as had the Antients' members before their 'union'. This stretch of Spilman Street has therefore been associated with the Craft for a much longer period than with any other aspect of the town's life. Parking one's car to reach the present hall may be a major problem but directing one's steps to this area of the town has been a practice of masons for nearly two centuries.

To return to the façade, one remarks that simple Doric pillars, again picked out in a lighter blue, separate the windows already mentioned whilst the entrance is flanked by two pillars of rusticated stonework, again in blue. Above the door is another pillared window suggesting already the anteroom that might meet one at the head of the stairs within. The whole frontage is completed with a simple flat band of pale blue stonework relieved by the thin line of decorated cornice. The whole is distinctive and inviting.

Within one at once recognises that here was a place designed at reasonable cost for brethren who knew what was needed. Of course the building has been adapted to new requirements, central heating, a more adequate bar and meeting

The chairs in the temple display a carved triangle and circle.

area in what seemed like the ante-room from outside, with a satisfactory dining room upstairs. Yet it is the ground floor rooms that first claim one's attention and which contain by far the most interesting features of this masonic hall.

On the right of the hallway as you enter there is a moderately large committee room with a table at its centre. To the left from its doorway is a bookcase filled with books and pamphlets belonging to the lodges meeting here and containing several items that would merit study by eager masons. Opposite this wall and running the whole length of the room to the recess beside the last of the street windows are a set of white framed cases. They are filled with items of masonic interest and objects linking this building with the Craft and other orders that are or were held in the vicinity.

It is as one surveys this intriguing, if not altogether well arranged, collection of masonic memorabilia that we might review a little of the past of Freemasonry in this town. Of its earliest beginnings we have already spoken and the interlude around the time of the Union has been mentioned but those are only two of the four stages through which Freemasonry here has passed. Definite and continuous masonic working in the town begins with the warranting in 1724 of a lodge No 34 which was to meet at the 'Bay Nag's Head and Star' in Dark Gate. In 1733 it removed to the Bunch of Grapes and was renumbered No 30 though its meetings then became more and more infrequent until it was replaced by a further Lodge, that of Perfect Friendship in 1753.

The interesting fact about the inauguration of this latter lodge was that it owed its emergence to a Sir Edward Mansell who in that very same year became W. Master of the Goose and Gridiron Lodge, one of the famous four lodges that came together to establish England's first Grand Lodge in 1717. It is now known as the Lodge of Antiquity No 2. What is so striking about this connection is that yet once again the Craft in Carmarthen is quite naturally linked with Freemasonry in the capital of England. It again underlines the surmise mentioned earlier that in some way Carmarthen and the wider world were significantly linked. To uncover that tie would be a piece of research that might prove of real benefit in several directions.

Yet to resume. This lodge started by Sir Edward was to last until 1777 when as Temple Lodge it was finally erased from the Premier Grand Lodge roll. Thence we hear nothing of local Masonry until the St David's Lodge of Perfect Friendship is created in 1811. That was to meet at the King's Arms in Priory Street.

After the Union Lodge had come into being it continued to serve local masons until 1829. This meant that pride of place in South Wales, Western Division, passed to St David's Lodge, No 366, of Milford Haven even though that lodge was warranted 10 years after the 'Union' here. It was to be members of the previous 'Union' lodge, however, together with the help of brethren in the Indefatigable Lodge of Swansea that finally formed the St Peter's Lodge which has maintained the standard of Freemasonry until the present day. Its celebration of 150 years of existence is an imminent festival which will no doubt be suitably honoured in this Hall.

There are jewels and collars and implements in the display cases, of this committee room which recall not merely some of this early period in Craft Masonry but aspects of masonic practice that have been practised here and now are forgotten or that were connected with members of Carmarthen lodges and left behind as tokens of their own past elsewhere. How else is it possible to account for home-made collars and sashes of the Knight Templar and Constantine and Rome degrees of which we have here such clear evidence? Might it even be that we have here also that remnant of connections with those

A selection of some of the prized jewels that are on display in the hall.

other orders in the town with which we know that some brethren were involved — the Ivorites and Oddfellows, the Loyal Order of Moose and the Royal and Ancient Order of Buffaloes — and which the Provincial Grand Lodge had to specifically declare as unacceptable associations for Freemasons to belong to? What would again prove to be of real local interest here would be a complete inventory of what these cases contain and the identification of each of the exhibits so that future generations of Carmarthen masons can appreciate the full measure of their local heritage.

Meanwhile there is here in any case a rich assortment of pottery and decorations, distinctive collars showing how our present forms of design came about, jewels of well known local men and aprons of differing styles. Herein is a past enshrined of which some who pass up and down the corridor outside have no knowledge whatsoever. For Masonry in general here are parts of our heritage that need to be better displayed and preserved.

To pass from here, through the corridor to the right and into the main lodge room is to move into a glorious present from a hazy past. All those who come to share in the ceremonies of this temple can do so in the full awareness of how much Freemasonry means to those who are the hosts in this place. Here is a room that displays to the full the richness of the care that has been bestowed upon its contents in the last 80 years and the attempt to create for those who enter it as candidates a real measure of awe and respect as they pass through their ceremonies.

Our eyes are inevitably led, as they should be, to the impressive arrangements of the east end of the temple. The Master's chair is one of a clearly designed set of three for the principal officers and the pedestals at the place of each are no less fine pieces of craftsmanship. The pedestal before the Master is particularly large and has an additional folding ledge in front of it for carrying the Volume of the Sacred Law on which the candidate will lay his hand. These pedestals are, moreover, enhanced by the delicate candlestick holders that rise beside each of them. With their chequered bases and their varied steps, three, two and one, they show an earlier generosity by some member of St Peter's Lodge. That this furniture came from the period when the lodge met in the hotel opposite seems certain for the design is clearly of more than a century ago. What is now so delightful is that unlike their use at the Ivy Bush the items can be left out constantly for any visitor to admire rather than put away after each meeting.

Of nothing is this more to be rejoiced over than the lofty white pillars that embrace the whole east end of the temple. By themselves they would be impressive but with their ancient globes, and those in their framed tripods, set on top of the pillars we have a feature that is worthy of any hall in Wales. What further supports the effect of these pillars is the matching furniture that stretches across the dais below thus giving to the whole end of the temple a sense of completeness and harmony.

In the centre of the floor are the tracing boards in their case and though these have nothing specially distinctive about them in terms of age and design yet they are obviously the boards that were acquired by this lodge of St Peter's when it began in 1841. Whilst remarking on their general uniformity of arrangement it will nevertheless be a matter for interest for any Master Mason to examine especially the second degree tracing board of any lodge he visits and compare its design with the one in his own lodge. He may be amazed to discover the great variety of arrangement that is there provided — either in the number of persons present, the number of chambers shown, the forms of character depicting 'God' or the number of steps on the staircase.

It is when one has examined the boards in this lodge room that one's attention may be peculiarly directed to the roof above our heads where the otherwise decorative ceiling is here pierced by a gloriously rich lantern that is not easily seen from the door on entry. In the midst of the lantern is a strikingly gilt 'G' hanging from a glory and the whole recess glows with the rich colours that surround it. The feature is all the more impressive for being so unexpected and shows once more how in halls that from outside might seem unduly modest and unspectacular there are constantly appearing architectural additions that make them both memorable and worthy of preservation.

Looking round this whole room, with its fine Masters' boards, the banners of its attendant lodges, Craft and Mark, the fine if simple organ, the distinctive deacons' chairs and the panelling which leaves one with a sense of warmth and intimacy, one cannot but rejoice to have discovered it and delight to know that yet again freemasons have a meeting place worthy of their ritual and redolent of their history. For this temple, like all the others that we retain, is not simply a museum. It is a home for those who continue the traditions of Masonry today. It is a home with a distinctive character, and bearing contents that make it the home of Carmarthen masons rather than those from elsewhere. It is a home of which both their forebears and themselves were and are properly proud.

Throughout this visit to the hall at Carmarthen we have followed a theme of linkage between Freemasonry in this town and the wider world of the Craft. Crossing the road from the present hall and standing at the entrance to the grounds of the present Ivy Bush Hotel one can still see the sections of the older building in which the St Peter's Lodge met before the end of the 19th century. There, in March 1856, an especial gathering took place 'to afford an opportunity of presenting to WBro F. Bolingbroke Ribbans, a very handsome testimonial, in the shape of some beautiful and useful domestic plate'. This presentation acknowledged one who had notably served the earliest Masonic Girls' School in London, the later Masons' Asylum, and his career in the Province of Limerick. Moreover Ribbans was connected in his early life with one Samuel Ribbans, Master of the British Union Lodge in Ipswich (see Ipswich: *Masonic Halls of*

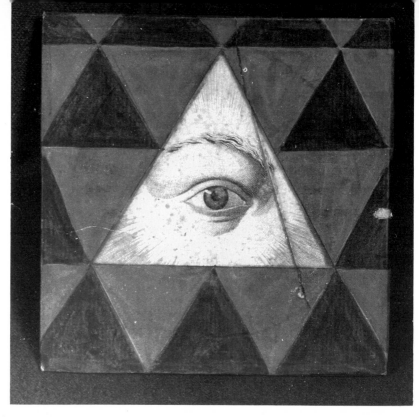

The painted All Seeing Eye is about 6in square.

England, the Midlands). By such diverse ways did this worthy brother find himself in the lodge whose hall we still have the pleasure and honour of visiting. Nor was that all. It was this man who was to be foremost in establishing a lodge in Llanelli — but that is another story altogether.

The ale jug, one side depicting Royal Arch and the other Knights Templar.

(CAERDYDD)

In the Land of Bute

NO ONE WHO today seeks to manoeuvre round the one-way system of the busy capital city of Wales, manages to park and visit both the grounds and the fascinating interior of the Castle at its heart, and then resumes his journey northwards past the restored walls and pinnacles of Castell Coch on the way to Merthyr Tydfil can possibly afford to be ignorant of the fourth Marquess of Bute. Though Cardiff was for centuries in the possession of the Earls of Worcester and its castle has a Norman foundation it is in the last 175 years that the real development of the city took place. That is the period of the Butes.

'Up to the latter half of the 18th century Cardiff was a small country town, unpaved, unlighted and without any organised system of sanitation. The Industrial Revolution began then to make its influence felt, and in 1821 the main streets were first lit by gas . . . The West Bute Dock was completed in 1839 and the East Dock in 1855. It was not until 1855 that the first train load of Welsh Steam Coal from the Rhondda reached Cardiff for shipment . . . The Taff Vale Railway was completed in 1841 and in 1858 the Rhymney Railway was opened . . . Until 1850 the Town Quay was in use in what is now Westgate Street (and) water was still obtained from wells. (For another decade moreover) the Town Hall was in the middle of the High Street and traffic passed on each side of it. There were 26 churches or chapels and of these 12 held their services in Welsh.' (*The Bute Lodge Centenary history.* 1963 p4.)

It was this steadily changing town that the Bute family was to affect with benefactions and building and it is hardly to be wondered at that the period of their influence should be marked amongst the masons by the formation of the Bute Lodge in 1863. It was not the first or only lodge in the area but it was to be one that lived up to the distinction of its name and was to make a significant contribution to the masonic life of the future city. Yet just because this new lodge was not wholly welcomed at first by its predecessor. the Glamorgan Lodge, No 43, we ought to turn to the earlier history of local Craft development here and understand the backcloth against which Bute Lodge appeared.

The earliest reference to Freemasonry hereabouts is made in a most intriguing document that is still carefully preserved and displayed in the present Cardiff Masonic Hall. It is a warrant issued in 1777 to some 'Bridgend Brethren' that was never actually despatched but kept in the hands of the Antients or Athole Grand Lodge. It was not in fact assigned to new and later Petitioners until 4 November 1808. That was the date on which certain brethren of the Caerphilly Lodge No 126 (which had begun but a year before) were assembled to start this first lodge in Cardiff. What is most to be noted is that by receiving this previous warrant the founders secured for Glamorgan a senior place in the Grand Lodge register and a seniority over Caerphilly in the Province.

Moreover, and just to confuse anyone who examines this ancient warrant further, there is an endorsement in its margin which states: 'This warrant is registered in Grand Lodges, Vol 1, Letter A, and bears the date 13 March 1753.'

The Masonic Temple at Cardiff also houses the Provincial offices.

This has led to some earnest masons of the past claiming for this old lodge an ancestry of even greater length. The fact is that this endorsement refers to the original issue of the warrant to other Antient Masons who had it before those to whom it now happily belongs. Yet even this date of 1753 is incorrect for we know that in that year there were only 27 Athole Lodges in existence and that it was only in 1754 that the number included '33' which was how this first Cardiff lodge was numbered. What probably happened was that when the warrant was handed over in 1808 the then Grand Secretary failed to do his homework correctly and 1753 was appended. To complete the story we need to know that it was not until 1811 that the lodge became known as 'The Glamorgan Lodge' and its number after the Union became 50, 43 and then 36 as it is today.

Such a document as this only further proves how full of history just *one* item in the present masonic hall can be and what a treasure house of study there is there for any diligent brethren. Not only are there displayed all the warrants of the masonic bodies that meet here but there are also several display cases in the main vestibule where a constant change of historic material can both interest and intrigue masons as they make a 'daily advancement in knowledge'.

The Glamorgan Lodge began its life at the Cardiff Arms Hotel, Broad Street, where it stayed for 47 years, and then moved to the Freemasons halls at Church Street (1855), St Mary Street (1859), and, when Bute Lodge had been formed, Working Street (1877). Whoever came up with the idea of the latter meeting place either had a sense of humour or a shrewd sense of what was appropriate for their venue. The Glamorgan Lodge flourished, as did the town, which in

1863 had a population of 33,000. One could hardly be surprised if in that year there was the move for another Cardiff Lodge.

As has been noted two new docks were now increasingly in operation and the desire for a meeting that would be held in the docks area was the real cause for the proposed Bute Lodge. Because Glamorgan may have felt that this might prove a threat to their membership or prestige as the sole masonic unit the encouragement looked for by the prospective founders was not forthcoming and so support was sought from the Silurian Lodge at Newport. A word from C. K. Kemys-Tynte, the Provincial Grand Master, however, soon brought a change of heart in the prior lodge and Bute Lodge was in fact petitioned for by the other Cardiff masons. Harmony did indeed prevail for a month after the consecration the Glamorgan Lodge records in its minutes that they were thanked for their support in obtaining the Bute charter and being asked 'if the lodge would lend them the harmonium at the opening ceremony of the Bute Lodge, this was unanimously agreed'. R. S. Fisher of Glamorgan Lodge had been in charge of the music on that important day of constitution, 6 Glamorgan men were in all the main offices and only the DC came from a Bristol lodge. The meeting place of the new lodge was to be the Consulate Chambers, Bute Docks. In the first 18 months the Charter Master, J. C. Thorp, initiated 76 brethren, including the Rev Nathan Jacob, Minister of the Cardiff Hebrew congregation. Those who today look at the tracing board case quietly tucked away in the new anteroom for the small temple here might reflect on the fact that in those early days of Bute Lodge there were given not only Lectures on the First and Second Degree tracing boards, but also 'an excellent and highly interesting lecture on the Third Degree' and a presentation by Bro Thorp and a team of new masons of the Seven Sections of the First Degree Lectures. It was clearly a case of more Masonry into men as well as more men into Masonry.

Almost 20 years later another lodge was founded bearing the name of a then greatly respected Deputy Provincial Grand Master called Marmaduke Tennant. He had been appointed Town Clerk of Aberavon in 1863 and at his death was to be the longest serving such officer in the kingdom. The Tennant Lodge was also to meet at Working Street with the Glamorgan but such was the popularity of masonry in Cardiff that by 1876 the Bute Lodge had found the Comsulate Chambers quite unsatisfactory and they too had proposed the formation of the Working Street Hall. With three lodges, all growing, now in occupation it is no surprise to read that in 1883 several meetings were held at the Queen's Chambers in Crockertown because alterations were having to be made at Working Street.

Finally, with such cooperation now established between the Cardiff brethren that in February 1887 there was held a joint Masonic Ball at the Park Hotel at which brethren could wear their Collars, Jewels *and* Aprons, it was decided in 1890 that it was time that Cardiff should have its own separate temple and a Committee was appointed to consider the matter. By April 1893 the committee was proposing that a sum of £4,500 should be offered to purchase the United Methodist Free Church chapel in Guildford Street, together with the school building attached to it. This Church had been granted a lease of the land by its owner, no less than the Marquess of Bute, in 1865 and it seems strange, if also providential, that after so short a period the chapel constructed on the site should be surplus to requirement. When one considers its dimensions it is hard to believe that it could have already become inadequate for its congregation. Be that as it may the three lodges were each consulted on the proposal and gave authority to the Joint Committee not only to conclude the deal but to take such steps as would be necessary to furnish and adapt the building for its new

The main entrance hall at Cardiff.

purpose. In the Bute Lodge there were immediate offers of £1,310 towards this venture.

A year later the Cardiff Masonic Hall Company Ltd was floated at the Working Street centre when the Certificate of the Registration of the Company was laid upon the table. That was 2 May 1894. In June subscriptions were invited for £4,000 in Debentures at £5 each and the share capital was to be wholly provided by the members of the Cardiff lodges. The first General Meeting of shareholders was called for 13 August and by 10 September the Directors of the Company were at last meeting in the Guildford St building. Thereafter the progress was steady and solid. On 14 February 1895 the Directors accepted a tender by Messrs E. R. Evans and Co to make the essential alterations to the premises for £1,500 and on 14 May they approved the tender of the Atlas Furnishing Company to fit out the Temple for £800.

As we shall see shortly a very special Master's chair was presented by the new Provincial Grand Master who had been installed in September 1894. This was Lord Llangattock who was to preside over the Eastern Division for the next 18 years. He was the only son of John Etherington Welsh Rolls (the family associated with Rolls-Royce) who had been Provincial Grand Master of Monmouth from 1863 to 1870 (See Monmouth hall). Not only is this devoted servant of Freemasonry ever to be remembered by the magnificent gift which he now made but in January 1895 there was also a new lodge consecrated bearing his family name — the Llangattock Lodge No 2547. This lodge was consecrated at the Working Street hall and was thus able to become another new tenant of the Hall Company. What may seem strange in the roll of Cardiff lodges is that Llangattock Lodge bears a later number and date of warrant than the Duke of York Lodge No 2453 which was warranted as early as 1892. A later explanation seems to have been that by the consent of the several founders it was deemed more fitting that the first lodge consecrated by the new PGM should be one closely allied to him whilst the Duke of York Lodge would have the special honour of being constituted in the new temple on the day of the latter's dedication and with the PGM now sitting in his *own* throne. It is also true that illness and delay in obtaining the Duke of York's consent to the use of his title also contributed to this order of events. At least the order of the lodges was thereafter restored to its proper sequence.

Before passing into the hall which was opened on 26 September 1895 it may be as well to complete the general story of its development up to the present. The furniture from the Working Street hall was purchased for £45, the two deacons' chairs for 8 guineas and two chairs for the dais at 10 guineas each. The Joint Committee which had represented the three older lodges became a corporate tenant of the Hall Company and paid an annual rent of £470. In June 1910 this Committee was finally dissolved and the separate lodges, now eight in number, together with the three Royal Arch Chapters and certain other masonic units became individual tenants. In 1904 the whole of the existing buildings were fitted for the installation of electric light at the expense of the Worshipful Master of the Duke of York Lodge, Isaac Samuel, and an 'illuminated' address was later presented to this generous donor. That seems to have been a very appropriate recognition.

In 1918 and subsequently the Directors, realising the continuing need for more accommodation in the years ahead, began to acquire the houses adjoining the temple in Guildford Street and that is why those on the left of the Hall's main façade as you face it are now the increasingly well appointed offices of both the Hall Company and the Province. By 1928 another adjacent site to the north of the vestibule had been developed and the New Temple was opened with a dining room suite above. It was dedicated by Edgar J. Rutter, the Deputy Provincial Grand Master-in-charge, and today it is generally referred to by his name. All the furnishing of this valuable addition was supplied by gifts from lodges and their brethren. Starting as we have seen with a very modest number of lodges and chapters the hall today serves 62 lodges and 23 Chapters, not to mention the Mark and other masonic orders. The home which they enjoy and which we are now to look at is both worthy of its first occupants and the Province of which it has become the centre.

Anyone who approaches the present hall down Bridge Street towards Churchill Way cannot but be struck by the tall and imposing grey façade that dominates the row of buildings across his path. Built in neo-classical style the frontage is topped with a parapet on which is now carved the description — MASONIC   HALL — and below this, two single and two pairs of lofty pilasters, with heavy rectangular pediments and indented but rectangular chapiters, flank five round headed window spaces, three in the centre and one each at the side. Each of the window heads has an arched band and a most prominent keystone, and this keystone motif is reproduced in a threefold form over what once was the central doorway of the chapel. It again has a rounded head and grooved panels over all its surface. When the building was previously used as a place of worship the windows were filled with glass (as may one day be again the case) and the doorway entered into the church building proper. Today the entrance is by a small pair of blue doors to the left of the frontage but this can easily be overlooked by those who must be impressed by this otherwise riveting pile. A closer look may reveal that renovation and repair to the lower string of plastered stonework may be necessary but the overall impression is that here is a hall worth visiting and one that cannot be easily forgot.

The entrance leads us through swing doors into a more human-sized corridor which connects, by a side passage to the left, with those offices that have already been mentioned. There are useful committee rooms and also, as a very recent addition, a modern, well furnished bar and recreation lounge replacing what were hitherto merely odd storerooms. Beyond these, however, and through yet another swing door we emerge into another section of the corridor with its well-kept parquet flooring, its fresh neo-Victorian decoration, showcases and stained glass. One senses already that we are in a building of character and tradition.

The showcases are filled with items that are changed from time to time and any wise mason will be advised to look over the aprons and other masonic regalia that are here laid out by the Hall Company Secretary. Yet just as fascinating and deserving of our attention is the array of masonic emblems that are portrayed in the panes of the swing door leading into this area as well as on the partitions and doors that lead one out of the corridor into the ante-room and old committee room to the right. Half of these areas are made up of well-preserved Victorian coloured glass and he will be a more knowledgeable brother who makes it his business to understand all the figures that appear in these surfaces. There must be about 40 to 50 of them in all. Whether these items came from the earlier halls or were made specially for this adapted chapel building is not known but it is a feature of unique quality and imagination and certainly makes this hall an immediate focus of interest. When to these illuminated panels you add the carefully framed and positioned warrants of most of the lodges and chapters that meet here you have a veritable storehouse of Cardiff masonic history laid out before you. One little clue to the possible antiquity of this decoration can be gained from the very first items that adorn the arched panel above the second swing door. The three emblems there are a beehive, an hour glass and a plain cross — not exactly the features that usually demand our explanation today.

Returning from the committee and ante-room we now find ourselves in what was obviously the old chapel hall for business or recreational activities. Today it forms a most useful foyer or vestibule where brethren can sit or talk together before or after meetings. Two tall round columns support the cavity-sectioned ceiling, their carved heads picked out in the same cream, yellow and light blue that also defines the grooved bases of each cavity. Decorated in a light cream colour throughout with a flood of light pouring in through the space created in one corner to receive the wide turning staircase there is a sense of freshness and space. The well-wrought, white balustrades of the ample staircase, with its useful chair-lift running up the wall-sides, is also decorated in each panel of white foliate ironwork with a bronze-coloured emblem of either a square and compasses or the Seal of Solomon. There are eight pairs of these up the staircase's length. Around the foot of most walls here as also around the base of one of the pillars there are well upholstered brown leather seats, and amongst these more black-framed showcases for items of local masonic interest. Here one can see some of the unused firing glasses of old, the range of keys used at the formal opening of the hall and its temples, old theatre bills for performances sponsored by masons, and various jewels of particular meaning as having belonged to Cardiff masons. One item of special interest in this area is a most delightfully carved oak tracing board holder which was obviously one of those used by one of the early Cardiff lodges but no longer required when the latest re-furnishing of the new Masonic Hall took place. It has been supplied with a glass top to prevent marking by drinks or cigarettes but its end panels with their square and compasses, the semi-circular and twisted rod stretchers, the strong but finely grooved legs, and the flower decoration around its four sides all make it a piece of hall furniture that has happily not been discarded.

It is from this vestibule that we turn first, through a newly partitioned ante-room, into the Lord Swansea or Small Temple. In a corner of the ante-room is another tracing board holder that has obviously seen better days. The boards that it once held for the Glamorgan Lodge have now been disposed of as worn out but their container is happily still with us. Its two end pieces, which support the box, are shaped as large levels with the pear-shaped globule near their base. The surface is interesting because when the appropriate board was placed on it the present remaining border of indented red and blue marking would complete the picture displayed.

The Small Temple into which we now pass has been tastefully but considerably altered from its earlier days. Gone is any semblance of the previous organ loft on the north side, any trace of the plain cornice that supported the cavity ceiling or the three shutters that dominated the east. Retained, however, are the two slender and gracious white pillars that flank the Master's chair in 'Oxford ritual' style, each surmounted by its appropriate globe. The pedestals and their chairs in a style like those of the 1895 Deacons' chairs form an elegant modern suite, the floor covering is both colourful and hard wearing, whilst the dais on which all the brethren are seated permits the flow of warm air in a manner that former generations would have envied. With brown and blue drapes behind the seats in the east, a hanging ceiling with its inset lights and yet the same polished brass 'G' that was hung there previously we have here an excellent example of how old and new features can combine to make a most useful addition to a hall that has to accommodate a vastly greater number of brethren.

The Edgar Rutter Temple at Cardiff named after a prominent local freemason.

The smallest of the three temples at Cardiff.

We pass now across the vestibule to the opposite corner and make our way by a curved passage area to the New or Edgar Rutter Temple. Here there is little that has changed though the room is so well maintained that it gives the impression of having been opened only recently. Here are the graceful wall brackets that support the cavity-sectioned ceiling, each area having a light at the centre of an eight-pointed gold and white coloured star. The room abounds in banners which bring colour and character to the whole and the dark blue drapes around the whole curve of the east end of the temple set off the pinky-cream colour of the main walls. In the east there is a large modern pedestal, paralleling those of the other Officers, and the chairs of the Master and Wardens are all of substantial size and quality. The Master's place is especially fine with its attendant white pillars and globes, a nine-feet high chair back set against a yellow curtain that brings out the rich grain of the wood and the rich blue material of the chair itself. This temple has been an enormous benefit to the users of this hall as being large enough for most lodge occasions and something less overpowering than the main temple to which we shall shortly move.

It ought to be said here that the brother whose name it bears has been something of a legend in these parts and was, by any masonic measure, a very distinguished brother. Initiated in Tennant Lodge in 1915 he became Provincial Grand Director of Ceremonies in 1928, Deputy Provincial Grand Master in 1931 and in the same year was appointed to the RMIB Board of Management of which he later became Chairman. In 1932 he was nominated by the Most Wor the Grand Master to a vacancy on the Board of General Purposes, served on all six committees of that Board, and in 1967 he played a great part in the Installation of the present Grand Master. He was the only person who so far has been Vice-President of the Board three times. He was also one of the first recipients of the Order of Service to Masonry in 1946, was the oldest holder of that distinction at his death, and in 1951 was made a Past Junior Grand Warden. As one passes out of this room's doors one cannot but feel that it is only right and proper that a mason of such service to the Craft and bringing such honour to his mother Province should have this noble room as his memorial for the future.

We cross the vestibule once more and passing through the lobby of stained glass already mentioned we enter the large Duke of Connaught temple which was, of course, the main body of the previous chapel. Looking down to the east we can make out the large round-headed doorway behind the Master's chair and the five round-headed windows above that were also part of the façade. These are the ones that it is hoped in due course to fill with frosted, shatterproof glass. In all the spaces formed by the original window areas and the walls between there now hang more of the many banners belonging to lodges meeting here so that there is a perpetual reminder of the whole masonic family to which those gathering here belong.

The loftiness of the dark-coloured ceiling with its light blue moulded cornice and central 'G' in a golden glory, the rich panelling of the lower wall areas, the banks of well-upholstered red armchairs and uprights all around the room and the huge indented and tasselled chequered paving set in a veritable sea of light blue carpet running right up to the dark blue dais seating on the sides — all this amounts to a Temple of distinction and grandeur. No-one who knew the chapel in its finest days could but be pleased that its subsequent use has been that of so fine a chamber. Yet besides these overall features there are two very special areas of the room that focus the visitor's attention. One is the central feature in the east and the other is over the whole of the west wall.

There, standing on a semicircle of the eastern dais, we see between two huge pillars that rise up to the level of the windowsills above, a most magnificent Master's chair. This is the piece that was mentioned as a gift from Lord Llangattock at the time of the hall's dedication to masonic purposes and in both dimension and decoration it is worthy indeed of its generous donor. Ample in its red-cushioned seating two fluted columns rise from the carved and heavily decorated arms and support at their heads the scroll work that leads to a shallow but richly ornamented canopy. This headpiece, with below what look like wooden tassels, has above its carved panels an array of neo-Jacobean scroll work supporting an oval medallion with an open raised square at its centre. Between the finial above it and those at the side there still stands that brass case, pierced with a star design at the front, which was once lit up to convey the idea of 'that bright morning star' of which at times mention is made.

Nor is this all. Beautifully executed on the rear, upper panel of the chair is a representation of the arms of the Rolls family with their singular motto 'Celeritas et Veritas' (Speed and Reliability), the arms being supported by a lion and a leopard, and surmounted by the coronet of rank with a helm and above a hand holding a baton. In the panel above the actual seat are the words 'Presented to the Masonic Hall, Cardiff, by the R Wor Bro Lord Llangattock.' and the date. To complement the chair there are two pedestals. One, for the Master's personal use, is large and heavy, with a curved front decorated with pillars and roundels holding masonic emblems. This is further attended by a smaller pedestal with huge red cushion which is used to bear the VSL and around which are curved red kneelers for the benefit of those who will kneel to make their obligations here. The whole ensemble is then rounded off by the rich brown pediments of the white pillars on each side, these pediments carrying the Seal of Solomon in gold within a circle. The heads of the pillars are richly moulded in gold leaf and bear their appropriate globes to complete them.

Standing in the east and looking towards the west one is no less impressed with the array of three large panelled arches (one of which contains the double-doored entrance) and above them the original chapel balcony which spans the whole width of the building. The old organ was also there until 1906 when the present instrument was installed in the presence of Lord and Lady Llangattock with a distinguished company of brethren and ladies. The cost of it was defrayed by the then existing Cardiff lodges assisted by a donation of 50 guineas from the Company's shareholders. The huge casing in brown oak with the delicate clusters of pale green piping towers above the whole room whilst the modern console to the right is so placed as to give the organist a clear

The magnificent Duke of Connaught temple. The Master's chair is flanked by two large pillars.

The ornate Master's chair was a gift from Lord Llangattock, son of John Rolls (of Rolls-Royce family fame). The arms of the Rolls family appears on the back of the chair with the motto 'Celeritas et Veritas' — Speed and Reliability.

view of the proceedings below. The winding staircase to reach it is also intriguing.

In old pictures of the temple we see that the pillars that now flank the Master's throne were once placed at the western end of the central flooring and just in front of them was the tracing board container that we met in the vestibule. Today the whole area is cleared and one can appreciate the vastness of the room. One is also able to see the golden pelican feeding its young in the centre panel of the western balcony. The secretary's desk has also been moved from its original place in the north east corner and now faces and balances the Junior Warden's pedestal. The desk itself is a gracious piece of Victorian furniture and with its contemporary rounded shade adds yet another touch of gracious dignity to this fine assembly hall.

It only remains to leave this temple and once more cross the vestibule to mount the stairs. As was suggested earlier the upper floor is given over to the dining areas and the kitchens but the No 2 Dining Room over the Edgar Rutter Temple is built in the same style as the room below with delicate ceiling cavities and fine window casements so that it is airy and spacious. The No 1 Dining

Room is even more grand with a fine cupola over the centre of the dining area, the windows around the base of the dome being picked out in floral designs of red, orange and blue and the eight sets of paired lights giving ample access for the sun during the day. There is also a stage at the side of the room so that this room can be used for entertainments on special occasions or ladies' nights. The whole upper floor is well maintained and a fitting conclusion to a tour of the hall.

Here then is the central meeting place of South Wales Eastern Division and it nobly reflects that distinction. Here is a hall fast approaching its centenary and well able to meet the needs of the century that will follow. The combination of the old and the uptodate, the sense of reaching back to 1777 and yet a readiness to meet tomorrow, rightly make this hall a proper source of pride to those who use it.

The original Chapel balcony now houses the pipe organ in the west of the temple.

CARDIGAN
(ABERTEIFI)

The Hall that was a Vicarage

IT IS BY no means an unusual thing to see a masonic hall formed from an earlier church building that is no longer required for its original purpose. Those who visit the halls at Caernarfon, Llanrwst or Narberth, to mention but a few, will see with what care and benefit such centres can be created. Yet the hall at Cardigan is perhaps unique in that it embodies the 'family aspect' of local church ministry in its present use as the 'family home' of Teifi Lodge. For the hall which we are to visit here was, until 1952, the vicarage of the local parish church.

As we can see the hall has an impressive appearance. Approached by a broad sweeping drive and the ample area for parking now made available the three storeyed house appears to be well decorated and maintained . . . though its upkeep is no small burden on the masonic bodies and their members who meet here. Framing the off-white plain walls of the frontage, with its strong central and gabled entrance projection, we note the rich blue down pipes and guttering as well as the strong blue roof edging that simulates an inverted square above the central gable. With the room and stairway windows also framed by grey-painted stonework — each with their own keystone — the effect is of tasteful care and nothing completes this sense more than the doorway through which visitors pass into its interior. Painted blue the doorway is also surrounded by grey-painted jambs and lintel and above it is a large roundel of white with a golden coloured square and compasses extended on a further blue ground. It is a vicarage no longer.

From its inception the Teifi Lodge had it in mind that when their finances were established and the opportunity offered there should be a serious endeavour to find a permanent home separated from other activities. The lodge was grateful to begin its life in the prestigious surroundings of the local Guildhall and as you look at the chairs, pedestals, candlesticks, columns, working tools, collars, wands and swords, not to mention all the other essential items for carrying out masonic ceremonial, right down to a silver salver and the organ, you are really looking at the generous spirit of those first men of the Craft in this Aberteifi lodge who each contributed some part of that vast array that we now take for granted. These were no less costly 70 years ago when they were first obtained and it is a tremendous tribute to those founders that within the first year each part of their lodge room was fitted out with everything that was essential.

Yet all these pieces of furniture and equipment had to be put away after each meeting in a large cupboard at the Guildhall and those who still engage in that operation elsewhere know how easy it is for items to be easily misplaced, damaged or just worn out by this constant dismantling and storage. It is no wonder that after one year the first step was taken of setting up a Building fund and three years later, in 1928, a small Committee was appointed to inquire into the purchase of a site suitable for the purpose. Many parts of Cardigan were examined but it was to be some time before a field was finally bought.

A parish rectory until 1952 when it became the home of Cardigan freemasons.

By 1931 it began to look as though the dream was to be realized for a field above the Napier Gardens in the town was obtained so that the freehold tenure of Parcbachpensarnau, an almost square area of 150ft by 148ft was available for use. Later on this site was added to by the purchase of an adjacent plot so that there was ample land for the erection of 'an ornate building with a reserve for development' (*50th Anniversary history*, p23).

Meanwhile, however, 'the draughty and cold atmosphere of the Guildhall' and the increasing inconvenience experienced by members in managing their lodge possessions meant that another home had to be found. One brother had now presented the central 'G' which adorns this lodge, the candidate's clothing had been presented as a gift from Kenwood Lodge No 800 USA and Edward Crawford Lloyd Fitzwilliams presented the two Deacons' chairs. It was this latter brother, a CMG and affectionately known as 'The Colonel', who also presented the lodge with one of its most attractive, as well as a most significant, adornments — the Lodge banner. This has an honoured place in the lodge room and the description of its design runs as follows:

'The first Eisteddfod in Wales was held in 1176, by LORD RHYS, Prince of South Wales, at his castle of Aberteifi, he having given a year and a day's notice of it. At this Eisteddfod he offered two Chairs (with valuable gifts as well) one to the Poet and the other to the Musician who would perform most skilfully before him. It was a young man from his own Court who won the victory among the Musicians, but the Bardic Chair went to the Province of Gwynedd, North Wales. This banner portrays the LORD RHYS presiding at that Eisteddfod. It is interesting to note that his body lies at St David's Cathedral in this Province.'

This description is on the reverse side of the banner. The motto that also adorns it — Hawdd cymod lle bo cariad — (Concord is easy where Love may be found) was but one of thirteen such sayings proposed and reveals the care and attention bestowed on what was to be a standard for others to follow in the generations to come. It is no wonder that the banner is greatly treasured by the members of Teifi Lodge or that their forebears wanted a proper and more permanent home for this and their other 'treasures'. It is also interesting to note that the citizens of Cardigan chose to invite the Royal National Eisteddfod of Wales back to its birthplace in 1976 to celebrate its 800th anniversary. A Past Master of the Teifi Lodge, G. Berwyn Williams was chosen by the town folk to be the Chairman of the Executive Committee and he was honoured by Her Majesty the Queen with the award of an MBE in the Jubilee Honours List of 1977 for his contribution to Welsh culture. The Rose Croix chapter here was named after Lord Rhys of Cardigan Castle.

In 1934 negotiations with Mrs M. E. Lewis meant that they could hire the Assembly Rooms at the Black Lion Hotel, Cardigan on an annual rent. What was now most important was that at last the lodge room could be laid out in its more or less normal order for most of the time and the burden as well as the wear and tear of constant packing-up was at last removed.

With the end of World War 2 which now intervened the local authorities were naturally eager to restore or extend the local amenities that had suffered restriction and neglect during hostilities. It cannot therefore have been surprising to a lodge that had for so long been the meeting place of those who were Mayors of the town — or even Sheriffs of the county — that 'public interest' should claim some of the land that had been obtained prewar for building a new hall. It was proposed to extend and widen the road at Napier Gardens to allow for easier access to what is now a residential estate and the lodge deserves the credit of both appreciating the public need and co-operating in making the land needed available at a proper cost. The remaining hope that a hall might be erected on the plot that was still to be theirs was in time shown to be an impracticable one and the members were to turn elsewhere for a solution.

One notes with interest that in 1950 a past Chaplain of the lodge, the Ven D. M. Jones, Archdeacon and a former Vicar of Cardigan, passed away and was warmly remembered by the Teifi brethren. Links with the local church community were thus personal and immediate and in January 1952, a General Meeting of the lodge was convened to consider a proposal from the Church Council of St Mary's regarding a possible new home for the lodge. This was that in exchange for £4,500 and the residue of the land still retained by the lodge elsewhere in the town the brethren should occupy with a freehold the Vicarage then belonging to that church. The vote was instant and unanimous and within a short time the Church Council intimated that they too were agreeable to the sale. It is worth noting that at the same time the Deputy Provincial Grand Master was another cleric, the Rev P. G. Wallis.

The sum required for the completion of the purchase was no small one at that time and the trustees were to have some anxious moments in the next few years about meeting the payments that had been incurred. Indeed a request from the South Wales Elecricity Board in 1955 to purchase a plot of land to the right of the house as you approach it was agreed for £50 and the Board were also allowed to have the land occupied by a thick hedge if they would put up a wall on the Vicarage side of it.

Even so the brethren clearly took pride in having at last a place that they could call their own. They arranged to have a caretaker and chose a new name for the place after holding a competition to find the best. They chose Plas-y-brodyr (The brethren's dwelling) and in 1954 the Rt Wor Prov Grand Master, Col G. T. Kelway, came to dedicate the new Temple. He commented afterwards that 'Teifi Lodge can really be very proud of their Temple, which has been so lavishly decorated and furnished.' As we shall see he had good cause to speak so feelingly about the accommodation that was now to become the home of not only the Teifi Lodge but in 1962 the Teifi Chapter and a decade later the Frenni Lodge. Eventually there was also to be a resident Mark lodge and a Roise Croix chapter. To maintain and justify such a fine building needed and still needs all the support it can get.

The entrance gates that first greet the visitor were constructed by Wor Bro Frank Foster in 1957 with the occasional help of other members, and Wor Bro D. J. Lewis undertook in 1960 to redecorate and improve the bar facilities downstairs. Another matter that occupied the attention of the Management Committee in 1964 was whether to convert all the lawn in front of the house into useful parking area but the majority felt that 'a little green is good for the eyes' and happily that decision has still been accepted and something of the original garden surround is still visible. It does help to make the premises look more like a 'home' and less like a mere club. A central heating system that was installed about the time of the Jubilee celebrations (1974) must have made those who attended here feel that it was even more a modern home than it was for those earlier occupants who had braced themselves to face the more inclement seasons.

It is time, however, to penetrate these walls which had now become the property of the Aberteifi masons. To do so is to get the same impression of space and freedom to move that is conveyed by the outside elevation but also underlines the mere cost of adequate heating and the labour involved in both decorating and cleaning such a hall. What is certain is that it could accommodate easily even more masons than those who presently use it and it is no surprise to learn that some of the rooms are occasionally let out to local groups who would appreciate such a local facility.

The downstairs area is fully utilised with dining, recreation and cloakroom or kitchen areas and from these there stretches up, in the main hallway, a large flight of stairs with a tall frosted glass casement window that stretches almost the height of two floors. One could well imagine here the effect of having the lodges' and chapters' emblems and mottoes set in stained glass as one approaches the temple and rooms above. As it is the place is full of light during the day and one mounts the turning staircase with eagerness to see how these brethren have at last disposed the many possessions which have come down to them during these first 70 years.

Turning to the left at the top of the stairs one sees two committee rooms each of them with their own distinctive array of contents. There are naturally some portraits of those men who first created the traditions of this place and whose names mainly occupy the bars that are figured on the Teifi banner. There is also the makings of a very useful library which began with John Rowland Daniel, a garage proprietor, who yet took 'his masonic duties seriously and conscientiously, at the same time preserving his sense of humour. His ambition was to add to the brethren's masonic knowledge by instituting a library in the Temple, and he was to some extent successful in that the Brethren contributed literature and volumes on Freemasonry.' (*Jubilee history*, p44). It has to be remarked that there were certainly some very original donations to the collection which merit the attention of the local brethren today, especially a complete set of the 'Little Masonic Library' published in Washington, USA, in 1924. It would also be good to see brethren still adding to this collection so that it was an even better ground for helping new masons to make their 'daily advancement in masonic knowledge'.

In these rooms also there is the making of a jug, mug and jewel collection which had its origin in the bequest of the masonic jewels beloning to Dr Selby Clare of Graystone House, Cardigan, who was first initiated into the St Peter's Lodge, Carmarthen, but was Worshipful Master here in 1926/7. He was certainly amongst the most well-known masons in the area and there are jewels here which reveal the extent of his interest. The pieces of pottery are not exceptional but they are of sufficient interest to awaken the attention of any masonic student who has never begun to look at such items before.

Most intriguing of all the exhibits in these rooms, however, is a remarkable framed and illustrated chart which again underlines the universal nature of the Freemasonry practised here. Flanking a central picture of clearly non-English design but bearing many symbols of common meaning, the document has six columns of manuscript which are divided into three pairs. In each pair of columns there are nine articles or clauses — one pair in Spanish, one in French and one in Italian. The articles all read the same in an English translation as follows:

1. Masonry has for its object the perfecting of man.
2. I pay respect to the Great Architect of the Universe.
3. Do good by loving that same God.
4. Listen to the voice of conscience.
5. Love your neighbour as you love yourself.
6. Do not seek to do to others what you would not want them to do to you.
7. Him whom you would protect another from, you should no less protect yourself from.
8. Do not thoughtlessly give vent to anger lest evil arise in a heart full of vice.
9. Avoid quarrels and insults and endeavour to be reasonable in all your doings.

This obviously admirable set of precepts is a feature easily able to be overlooked in such a large building and there is no indication as to its origin. One can only assume that it may have been brought home by a Master Mariner member, like John Lloyd Richards, who had for many years pursued his business in great

The temple room at Cardigan is compact. The pillars in the east are richly gilded.

waters. The memory of him as one known for his uprightness of conduct and his long service in later years on the Cardigan Borough Council would well suggest that such a seafarer, having the contents of such a chart made known to him or even acquiring one of the languages concerned, would want it to be displayed in his masonic home here. He was Master in 1932.

We now come to what is so often the pièce de résistance in any masonic hall, the temple itself, and here there is no exception. Leaving the landing and passing towards the rear of the house we enter an almost square room with pleasant wood panelling up to a height of about 7ft around the whole wall-area. This tends to make the room seem smaller and more homely but it also gives a sense of warmth and certainly sets off the numerous items which the room contains. The outer edge of the ceiling is blue and matches well the blue curtaining of the two windows and the blue background of the three banners that hang on the east and south walls.

The Teifi Lodge banner has already been described but the Chapter banner and the one for Frenni Lodge are no less attractive. The former of these last two, besides bearing the pentagram with TH at its heart above and a representation of a Castle gate and portcullis at its foot, has a lovely seascape in an ellipse at its centre, showing a motor trawler crossing the waves as the sun is setting on the horizon. The whole banner has Royal Arch chevrons at its side from top to bottom. The Frenni Lodge banner shows an attractive rural scene of a river with cattle in the meadows alongside, and in a scroll that runs around and beneath a cushion with the Volume of the Sacred Law are the words of one of those other mottoes that was discarded by the Teifi Lodge in 1924. The words are: Gwnau gyfiawnder ac nac ofna (Do justice and fear not).

Most of the ceiling, however, is lightly recessed and covered with a fawn coloured paper that in turn matches the woodwork and from the edge of one of the air vents in this expanse there hangs the G that was presented by Llewellyn

The Teifi Lodge banner depicting the first Eisteddfod in Wales in 1176.

Davies. Exactly matching this recessed area above we have one of the lodge's real objects of pride — a black and white carpet set in a surround of deep Tyrian blue. The carpet would do honour to any lodge room and is not only remarkable for the freshness of its appearance and the perfect way in which it fits this temple but also for the workmanship displayed in its execution. The four knots and tassels at the four corners are probably the largest ever made for a floor carpet and the surrounding chevrons are themselves bold and deep. It is a perfect example of its kind and replaced the original lodge carpet which was bought by the Province in 1959 for £16.

This fine floor covering naturally leads one's eyes to the east end where, between the two Teifi banners, we see a fine arrangement of features around the Master's Chair. The original pedestal, like its partners for the Wardens, is of real craftsmanship, with two miniature pillars in semi-relief on a base and supporting the graded pedestal top. In the centre of the front face is a grooved square with a charming and clasped ornamental belt within it and inside that the appropriate emblem for the officer who sits behind it. These pedestals, like the equally fine candlesticks that are attached to them, show the effects of considerable care and maintenance. They are bright and well polished so that the equally matching columns that adorn the Wardens' places are in no way unfitting. The chairs behind the pedestals were again almost certainly made to measure and they all have beautifully padded backs, pillared frames, headboards that carry again the appropriate emblem and a little emblem in gold that signifies the state of the sun for each place. The steps of three, two and one to each chair are also perfect.

Of matching elegance and far outdoing even the comfortable tip-up chairs in which the rest of the Past Masters sit are the two Deacons' chairs at the north east and south west corners of the room. They are chairs that would outstrip even the Master's chair in many another lodge room for they are of some antiquity, have an abundance of carving throughout and are elegantly upholstered in red leather with arm rests in the same. Their donor, of whom we read earlier, must certainly have been glad to see such items left in their place and not constantly handled into a 'safe place' and the officers who occupy these seats must surely feel that they are being well prepared for the august places that await them next in their progress up the ladder.

Finally, in this charming apartment, we must remark on the two large golden pillars with differing chapiters and globes that were constructed in 1966 by Haydn Davies. They again illustrate the Oxford Working instruction as we will see at Fishguard and their positioning all the more adds to the other feature between them and over the Master's place. This is a triangular pediment supported on two much more slender red columns which have the design of the Seal of Solomon at their head. When these columns thus adorned are seen in relation to the archway between them, with red and gold stripes decorating the rear wall, one is forcibly reminded of the close relationship of Craft and Royal Arch.

Such is the central and most memorable feature that nowadays transforms this once no doubt happy clergy home into a place of equally happy masonic brotherhood. That keeping up such a large hall in so comparatively a modestly populated area is a constant task no-one can overlook. Yet the brethren here have more than fulfilled the longings of those brethren who went before and who, though they may never have seen the present building with their own eyes, can at least rejoice to know that their gifts of yesteryear are now properly used and valued and bringing delight to all who can now visit and know about Plas-y-brodyr.

FISHGUARD

(ABERGWAUN)

Kemes Lodge built to Order

THE NORTH COAST of Pembrokeshire is steeped in history and the port of Fishguard has no little share in that past. Its very lay-out in two distinct parts, the Upper and Lower Town, indicates some of the changes in its fortunes and a wander round both will provide interest for both the tourist and the student. Lower Town lies several hundred feet below at the mouth of the Gwaun Valley and here will be found the old harbour with its ancient quay and old fishermen's cottages, not to mention the old granary building that reflects the same trade as that mentioned in the chapter on Haverfordwest. This town area was bombarded by the infamous American Scottish 'pirate', Paul Jones, during the American War of Independence. More recently it was to be the location for the filming of Dylan Thomas's verse epic *Under Milk Wood* when this became his imaginary 'Llaregub'.

The Upper Town developed, with nearby Goodwick, as both the roads were improved and the railways reached the area. In the Royal Oak Inn at what might be called the town centre today we can read a tablet that records how in this hostelry the Irish/American Col Tate signed the famous surrender terms following an abortive attempt at the invasion of Britain by his 1,200 French 'convict' troops in the period of the French Revolution. That was 1797. Yet Fishguard was not for some time to enjoy the prosperity or position which was enjoyed by Haverfordwest and it was to that town, and to the Cambrian Lodge after its inauguration in 1840, that those who would enjoy Freemasonry had to make their way.

Writing in the history of the Kemes Lodge which was to be established in Fishguard in 1906 G. Oliver Davies, JP describes how those Victorian freemasons travelled to the county town 'in those early days by "shank's pony", dog-cart, trap or horse-drawn bus; later on they aspired to motor-cars, their path lighted by oil lamps. The sixteen miles to Haverfordwest was a day's journey. An attempt to travel from Fishguard to Haverfordwest and return the same day was a hazard not to be lightly undertaken, yet on more than one occasion our (founder) Secretary had to make the journey to meet the Deputy Prov Grand Master, WBro the Rev Canon Bowen, to make the arrangements regarding the Consecration.'

The founding of the Kemes Lodge in Fishguard was itself a local masonic milestone. There had been no consecration of a lodge since 1883 in the Western Division of South Wales and yet Freemasonry in the country as a whole was growing apace. With so vigorous a countrywide patron as Edward, Prince of Wales, the later King Edward VII, it was hardly to be imagined that anything else would be the case.

It was on 24 August 1905 that the first gathering of freemasons living in Fishguard came together to consider a possible and separate lodge there. They met at the County School and C. Cuthbert Thomas and Tom Matthews were elected Chairman and Secretary respectively of the new committee. Prominent members of the Cambrian Lodge at Haverfordwest were to be interviewed to

Although giving the appearance of being a church, the hall at Fishguard was purpose built in 1924-26.

see if they would join or give their support to the proposed lodge and it was at this stage unanimously agreed to call it the 'Abergwaun Lodge' for obvious local reasons. Abergwaun is the Welsh, and Fishguard the Norse, name for the locality.

The committee were also charged with finding a fitting meeting place and first thought that a Mr Jackson's bungalow would be suitable. Not being able to get reasonable terms agreed with the owner of that property they looked at the cottage by the Tan yard but that too had drawbacks that ruled it out. They were thus driven to look at some rooms above a Mr Davies' shop in West Street, which was later to be the premises of Messers A. and E. Nicholls. All this was being reported in August.

By October the Fishguard brethren had made a much bigger step forward. They had obtained the full backing and sponsorship of the Canbrian Lodge members and J. C. Yorke was offering to present them with a building site having a frontage of 25ft for the purpose of constructing their own Masonic Hall on the Brodog land. The offer was most gratefully accepted. To show that their eagerness and gratitude was not only heartfelt but practical all the new lodge members agreed to become security for a sum of £5 each. In 1906 that was quite an undertaking. It was also agreed to order lodge furniture which was described in the catalogue as 'the second class No 2'. Those who see the chairs and pedestals of the Master and Wardens today can now perceive what was being offered to lodges as standard equipment at the start of this 20th century.

When in February 1906 Francis Davies rejected the agreement for renting the rooms above his shop and the Grand Secretary had suggested that another name for the new lodge be found the members might reasonably have felt that the tide of easy success was beginning to ebb. However, another name known locally, that of KEMES, was accepted by London, and the Brodog site having already been marked out it was agreed that a temporary hall should be erected for use whilst the larger and more permanent one was constructed around it. By March the move towards their goal could be resumed. It was now that the question was raised as to whether the lodge proceedings should be conducted in Welsh but as there seemed to be some difficulty in obtaining a ritual in Welsh this idea was abandoned. To many living on the mainly Welsh speaking side of the Landsker Line that decision must have been a severe disappointment but it did mean that anyone coming to live in this area, not least in retirement, could join Kemes Lodge whatever their mother tongue. At least the die was cast and with this decision the committee wound up its work.

It was on Friday, 20 April 1906, in the County School at 1pm that Kemes Lodge was formally consecrated and constituted. The previous Chairman became the Worshipful Master and the Secretary remained the same. The Secretary, Tom Matthews, MA, was one of the first Assistant Masters at the Fishguard County School and he could certainly have appreciated the work being done in his native tongue. He was exceedingly interested in Welsh language and cultural matters and is recorded as having spent most of his holidays in Rome collecting information regarding early Welsh history.

The list of initiates in the first three years very clearly indicated that Freemasonry in the neighbourhood was well established in the community for it included the local auctioneer, Owen Gledhill, BSc, another County schoolmaster, the Harbour Master, an engine driver, the Berthing Master, a bank manager and two of his cashiers, and the Inland Revenue officer. Moreover it was significant that at a time just following the great Revival in Welsh Nonconformity (1904) and when Welshmen were beginning to be highly effective in national political affairs, men could gather in such a new lodge as Anglicans, Methodists or Calvinistic Independents on the one hand and as landowners, conservatives and trades union members on the other and still enjoy the fraternal fellowship and common purpose of a local lodge meeting.

It was in 1907 particularly that the lodge began to acquire those items that give a specially distinctive flavour to the temple of the present building. A minute for 18 January records:

'Bro Matthews then presented to the Lodge two framed "Remembrances" which he had been deputed to so present by Bro Levi Thomas. Bro Thomas was unable to be present and had received these (items) from Bros Ribbe and O'Donovan, the Grand Orator and Grand Secretary of the Lodges of Marseilles in 1877. A vote of thanks was then proposed . . .'

The items underline the continuing link between this part of the country and the French, albeit these documents (as illustrated) suggest fraternal and warm-hearted relations and serve to emphasise the bonds which in the Craft surmount merely national allegiances. They indicate a kind of European association of which 1992 will make us all, as simple citizens, more and more

As with other halls in Wales, Fishguard possesses a substantial pair of pillars with globes. It is a feature of Oxford *ritual working for these to be placed either side of the Master's chair.*

aware. The fact that the 'Remembrances' come from Marseilles, another port, is especially appropriate for Fishguard with what was then a developing harbour there. It was to be such a harbour as the great SS *Mauretania* was to use in 1911 on one of its cross-Atlantic journeys.

In this same year the question arose of purchasing a banner and the Worshipful Master contributed almost half the sum required for obtaining the fine standard that they desired. The one gracing the lodge room today was made as an exact copy of the former by the nuns at St David's. It is worth noting the change in money value by remarking that the finished product then cost just 12 guineas. The arms on the banner are a differenced adaptation of the arms of Warren, a local family whose arms are quartered with those of the Lords Kensington. It was one of the latter who consecrated Kemes Lodge and laid the foundation stone of the present building. This banner was to be joined much later by that of the other lodge meeting here, that of Strumble Lodge, No 4351, founded in 1921.

In the new showcase of local items of masonic history that has now been started in this masonic hall the year 1907 is again marked by the fact that it was then that the Founder Master, Cuthbert Thomas, was presented with the first jewel for the lodge that was newly formed. That Royal Arch Masonry followed promptly on the heels of Kemes Lodge's formation is also shown here and it is very encouraging to see the present occupants of the premises accumulating these distinctive memorials of the past as it steadily moves towards the centenary of its existence.

The large tracing boards are placed centrally in the temple.

That showcase also contains the boxed Presentation Key that was handed to the Masters of Kemes and Strumble Lodges by F. Langford, the grandson of the Deputy PGM who had graciously agreed to open the new and more permanent Temple in November 1925. The whereabouts of this key had for long been uncertain but in 1985 Langford casually met one of the Kemes brethren and then made an offer of letting them have this key on loan for as long as it was needed for display. It is another fine addition to the growing collection.

In 1909 the needs of the Kemes Lodge were such that it was felt to be necessary to extend the temporary building, and though some work was undertaken the advent of wartime limitations and reduction of resources meant that only a few changes came before the war was over. In 1916 Bro James Thomas presented the lodge with an iron gate and two stone pillars for an entrance to the walled surround that had been constructed on this previous site. That was the year that marked the death of W Bro Thomas and it was through his will that the lodge at last acquired a sum of £30 which was granted for the purchase of the two lofty pillars that stand so prominently to this day on both sides of the Worshipful Master's chair in the lodge room that was soon to be built.

Steps were now taken towards this goal of a new and final temple by receiving from W Bro William Evans the deeds relating to the grounds occupied by the lodge. This action in 1920 meant that the lodge was now free of all legal charges respecting the said property and could begin to consider its further development. The idea was given further impetus when it was agreed in 1921 to create another local lodge with the name 'Strumble' and intended as the focus of membership for those who lived in the Goodwick area across the bay and below Pen Caer and Strumble Head. The new temple was to be the home of both masonic bodies and would benefit by the increased income coming from a larger membership. Kemes Lodge even added to the possibilities of using the new Hall by also registering as a 'Social Club'.

In 1924 the new building committee met for the first time in June, and by 5 December the Rt Hon Hugh, Baron Kensington, Provincial Grand Master, was conducting the ceremony for laying the foundation stone. It was to be February 1926 before the dedication of the completed building could be arranged, but at last there arose the fine and stately detached building which members and visitors can attend at today.

It is not surprising that some who come to the hall nowadays might imagine that this was a previous church or chapel structure for it has all the appearance of having been such. The very fact that there is so much parking space all around it suggests that this was a gathering place for worship previously but it was in fact the foresight and good fortune of the earlier masons which has now ensured that meetings here can be so easily attended by the many who use a car for the purpose. Certainly the hall, with its clearly marked name on the façade, is not easily overlooked.

One passes through the simple iron gate already referred to and is confronted with a tall gable end to the sides of which, at half height, are attached two side rooms with their sloping roofs. In the centre of this wall before us is the entrance porch with a two panelled doorway recessed and guarded by two stone pillars of about 10ft in height. They support a heavy stone pediment, with a triangular course of stone above it, and that in turn surmounted by an arched window with two upright supports and five symbolic keystones cut into the plain face of the surrounding area. Finally, at the sides of the gable are two symbolic pillars, in only partial relief, with some kind of modernistic moulding at their head. The whole suggests that without any attempt at either classical perfection or undue ostentation the whole has been designed to convey some of those ideas that mean something only to the brethren who enter the building for their ceremonies. Seven windows, five keystones and three sets of pillars must surely have been meant to say something.

We pass into a commodious entrance hall, off which we can move to the ample facilities for catering and dining but especially by a long direct staircase to the rooms above. In the far corner of the present dining room is the display case of which mention has been made already and besides the items already referred to are a plastic charity jewel made for use in 1944 in wartime and attached to the breast by a simple safety pin; the PM's jewel given to the first Master of Kemes Lodge and eventually returned from Australia; a rather different jewel of an Enthroned Commander in the Royal Ark Mariner degree as well as a 'Coracle' RAM jewel for a 50th anniversary; and a fine masonic quart jug with many different designs on both its faces. Already this hall is acquiring a local sense of real history which will be all the more appreciated when Kemes brethren reach their Centenary in 2006.

On the first floor reached by the stairway one is first aware of a sense of spaciousness and ease of movement in what is after all a country masonic hall.

A magnificent glass goblet enriched with many masonic symbols.

Here there is none of that frequently met restriction on space which may have been borne by the previous masons of the area but ample provision for robing, with two large committee rooms. In one of these there is a glass fronted cabinet which contains a modest but still useful selection of books that can assist any brother here who wants to make his daily advancement in masonic knowledge. Here too will be found one of the framed 'Remembrancers' that have been already described, with its certificate issued by the Grand Orient of France in 1878 but in masonic cypher. The unravelling of this item would be a most worthwhile undertaking for some local student to tackle.

We pass at last into the lofty and well maintained temple that forms the core of this new 65 years old hall and can see, as we look round it, the marks of that lasting attachment and interest in local Masonry that makes even the most ordinary masonic meeting place a matter for some interest and attention. Here we see the central carpet that replaced the original chequered one used from the lodge's inception. This one is already 45 years old. There is the newer organ that replaced an earlier one provided for the sake of the musical items that distinguish masonic ceremonies here. There is the clock now in the dining room presented by Strumble Lodge for joint use with Kemes but which was given to commemorate that moment when three blood brothers occupied in the same year the three principal offices of Strumble Lodge.

Yet the most striking feature of the whole room is the pair of tall painted pillars that flank the Master's place. Costing £22 when they were installed after the new temple was erected they were ornamented in their present form by Charles Morris, who was Master of Kemes Lodge in 1947. Standing on two firm plinths which are decorated with two crossed squares and compasses, the two shafts are capped by two different forms of moulding, Doric and Ionic, and support at their head two symbolic and carefully drawn terrestrial and celestial globes.

These pillars, that so forcibly draw the attention of a visitor and must surely impress themselves on the mind of any new made brother when he at last comes to light, are also indicative of the working which was adopted by the Kemes Lodge at its foundation when, it may be recalled, a Welsh form of ritual did not prove possible of adoption. This working is called *Oxford* and is the one used in at least three other centres hereabouts. In that form of masonic working the Explanation of the Second Tracing Board has the following sentence:
'Every Mason's Lodge has or ought to have two columns, one on each side of the Master's chair: these are intended to represent the pillars at the entrance of the Temple.' One must wonder what West Wales masons who visit many English lodges feel when they see this symbolism far from being obeyed. Here at least they have the words brought visibly to life.

Reflecting upon the symbolic lighthouse which adorns the banner of the Strumble Lodge, the light and airy nature of this fine lodge room and the candelabra that graces every Installation table as a token of remembrance for the 50 years of Freemasonry experienced by WBro G. Oliver Davies of the Kemes Lodge a visitor might care to be reminded of some words used in the address at the laying of the foundation stone of this very building.

'I would not give much for your Freemasonry unless it can be seen – Lamps do not talk, but they shine. A lighthouse sounds no drum, it beats no gong, and yet far over the water its friendly spark is seen by the mariner. So let your actions shine out your Freemasonry. Let the main sermons of your life be illustrated by your conduct, and it shall not fail to be illustrious.'

Those who were present on that occasion and were bringing to fruition the hopes and longings of an earlier generation of Fishguard freemasons did indeed

62

One of the fine decorated masonic jugs to be found at Fishguard. This one depicts symbols, some of which are no longer seen.

set a light in motion that present members and their guests can both savour and maintain. Whilst this hall may not be a lavish treasury of many masonic possessions of great antiquity or value yet it has already a past to be proud of and enough history to preserve. It is not only the neighbourhood that is redolent of the past. Here too is a heritage in which both Kemes and Strumble Lodge members can take pride.

HAVERFORDWEST

(HWLFFORD)

A public meeting place

WHEN IT IS realised that the Norse word 'vik' meant a creek or small cove it is surely no surprise to learn that the inland waterway with Haverfordwest at its head was probably first named by a group of Viking pirates. It was certainly in the 8th century that people from Scandinavia came and settled at this bridging point and gave it the name 'Haver fjord' (Harbour inlet). It was soon to become a prosperous and historically important trading centre and being geographically very much in the heart of Pembrokeshire it is no less surprising to note that it is also the county town. It received the first of its many charters in the 12th century and in the Middle Ages was probably the largest town in Wales.

In the 12th century too Gilbert de Clare, 1st Earl of Pembroke, built the still formidable looking castle here in order to protect the English settlers from their Welsh neighbours to the north. Happily the castle has now been converted into the County Records office, an Art Gallery and Museum. St Mary's Church in the High Street further reflects the town's lucrative past and the fact that there are two other fine church buildings in the vicinity also shows the importance of the place. 'Haver fjord' was a 'Corn inlet' and this was for centuries part of its purpose. Hanover Quay was once full of large warehouses used for storing corn produced in the surrounding countryside or wool from farther afield in West Wales. The town also boasted paper mills, ironworks and a small shipyard, as well as some fine merchants' houses along its busy streets.

It will therefore seem in no way odd that it should be here that the second earliest lodge in Wales was formed. Moreover, considering the fierce trading rivalry that existed between Tenby, Pembroke and Haverfordwest it was natural that the name of the first lodge started here in 1741 was 'Tyrian' with its usual symbol as used in other 'Tyrian' lodges extant today — a Greek sailing ship with its banks of oars. This lodge was erased in 1773 after having met, again most appropriately, first at the Ship and Castle in the High Street (under the craggy eminence on which the castle sat) and then at the Three Cranes.

The next mention of masonic activity locally is of the Hwlffordd Lodge, No 23 in the Antients' Grand Lodge register, which met first in a private room, and then subsequently at the Blue Boar in Dew Street or the New Inn, Market Street. Though this lodge only lasted 16 years its membership perfectly reflected the nature of the town at the time. We are told that as this port thrived it also acquired a notorious reputation for turning a 'blind eye' on the many forms of plunder brought by pirates or other mariners who infested the Western approaches and preyed on unfortunate merchantmen. The first Master and Wardens of Hwlffordd Lodge were from Bristol lodges whilst other founders came from Halifax (the wool connection?), Manchester, Newfoundland, Scotland and Newport, Gwent. Haverfordwest was certainly a place where men from many parts came by sea to do business.

Just a decade after the closure of Hwlffordd Lodge a move was made to revive Freemasonry in the town by seeking a warrant for the Cambrian Lodge No 683. It was constituted on 27 January 1840 and though its founders were now much

more locally based they still planned to meet at the Mariners' Arms. The Master-designate was even described as 'of late No 81 (Hwlffordd)' and a former Junior and Senior Warden of the older lodge also joined at the first meeting after the constitution of Cambrian. There was a removal of the lodge to the Castle Hotel from 1854 to 1866 but they were back at the Mariners thereafter. What is worth noting is that with the arrival of the railway in 1853 the sea trade of Haverfordwest steadily decreased and the county town began to settle into its present role as an adminstrative and distribution centre. When the lodge began to experience a revival in 1864 its first new member was John James, holder of a number of clerkships (not sailing ones) and the Secretary and Actuary of the local Savings Bank. It was from such town worthies that the first Trustees of the newly projected Masonic Hall Company were drawn.

The first public intimation that we retain of this new venture amongst Haverfordwest freemasons is the issue of a 'Preliminary Announcement' on 16 December 1868 and signed by no less a person than the same John James. Bearing the unmistakable masonic emblems of an 'all-seeing eye, a square, open compasses and between them a circle with a centrepoint, and the level, plumb and open dividers' this leaflet for public distribution announced:

'A GRAND MASONIC BAZAAR
will be held in this town during a Hunt Week, 1869
Under Distinguished Patronage,
in aid of the funds
FOR ERECTING A MASONIC HALL IN HAVERFORDWEST
Further Particulars Will Shortly Appear'

As can be seen the Craft was then very much more in the general public's eye than is the usual case today. The lodge members, as has been stated, were prominent in the everyday life of the town and its government and they were very conscious of the fact that, quite apart from wanting a more permanent home for their swiftly growing lodge (60 members added in six years) there was no adequate public assembly hall with reasonable acoustics and such amenities as would enable concerts, Balls and other larger functions to be held locally.

The matter had been a subject of complaint by the local newspapers for several years so it was in no sense a private ploy to suit the Masons' own book which now led to more vigorous action to deal with the lack. The lodge might benefit but only with the public's great need in mind. This was even more evident when the members of the public learned the terms of the lease granted to William Saunders, Governor of the Pembrokeshire County Gaol and also W Master of the Cambrian Lodge. It was a lease made in July 1688 for 99 years, at a nominal rent of £1 a year, and was granted by the Rev James Henry Alexander Philipps, a son of Picton Castle, who was also then Vicar of St Mary's and who was initiated in Cambrian Lodge on 1 February 1869. The fact that he seems to have progressed no further in the Craft suggests that he may have been so admitted in order that at least he could take a proper part in the eventual consecration of the building that was to arise on the site he had granted, though it is also true that he died in 1875.

The lease on this plot of 40ft by 83ft in Picton required that the executors, administrators and assigns as named should erect and completely finish, before 29 September 1872, a good and substantial masonic hall or lodge room for use only as such, or as a Concert and lecture room or for similar public purposes, but

Haverfordwest Temple room.

for no residential purposes saving those needed for a caretaker. Significantly it was also prevented from being used as or for a Roman Catholic church, Nonconformist chapel or Dissenting meeting-house. As a result it seems to have been a singular coincidence that the Roman Catholic church in Dew Street was built in 1871 and consecrated in May, 1872.

The Master of Cambrian Lodge and 14 other members were assigned the lease as Trustees on 19 January 1870 and it was further required that any future Trustees had to be subscribing members of the lodge, their numbers to be made up when they reached only five, and such vacancies only to be voted on when the lodge members present contained at least two-thirds of brethren who lived in Haverfordwest or Pembrokeshire. Besides the Worshipful Master, William Saunders, the first Trustees included the Rev Thomas Gwynne Mortimer of Castlebythe, Thomes Rule Owen, the Land Agent, 2 Solicitors, 2 Solicitors' clerks, a Bank Manager, a chemist, jeweller, ale merchant and grocer, not to mention Richard Lewis, the Superintendent of Police. Their task was 'to build a Masonic Hall . . . at the expense of the members of Cambrian Lodge or such other persons or bodies as shall think fit to subscribe to the same . . .' It was this latter clause that led to such undertakings as the 'Grand Masonic Bazaar'.

Strange to say the lodge minutes at this time of such important decisions are completely silent on what was actually taking place. No plans or drawings have been found though it is reliably believed that the architect was a George Morgan of Carmarthen and one can hardly quarrel with a designer bearing such a name. The fact that he also planned and built a large chapel in Carmarthen in 1879 with a façade incorporating Corinthian pillars of Bath stone not unlike those in the frontage of the hall at Haverfordwest does seem to confirm that what he had found to be publicly acceptable in the latter town was no less likely to find favour in the former. 7 masons and 8 labourers were used at the height of the work.

What are indeed mentioned in the lodge minutes from 1869 are the steps taken to provide financial backing for the project by the lodge members. In August it was resolved that £25 be taken from the lodge funds and granted to the Masonic Hall Fund, and not surprisingly, since John James was the secretary involved, the fund was to be invested in the Pembrokeshire and Haverfordwest Savings Bank. The lodge members were also issued with collecting cards though how much they raised by this means is not known save that in the final account we have £200 from 2 'concerts, members' collections and public donations'. Far and away the largest single item in raising the money required was the £400 that came from the Bazaar which took place on 18 to 20 November 1869. The most encouraging thing about this occasion was that though the event was wholly organised by known freemasons yet the public gave it their complete support, partly or chiefly because of the public need which was being satisfied.

'The list of patrons, patronesses and stall-keepers, reads like a local 'Who's Who' and is headed by the Hon Col Edwardes, MP for Haverfordwest, who was initiated in Cambrian Lodge the day before the Bazaar . . .' He later became Lord Kensington and was Master of Cambrian Lodge in 1878 and Provincial Grand Master in 1885. Other patrons were the Prov Grand Master of the time, Sir Pryse Pryse, Bart, Thomas Meyrick, another MP, the Deputy PGM, the Revs J. H. A. Philipps and T. G. Mortimer and other town notables. On 17 September the Editor of the local 'Herald', having seen the plans and

Fitted Working Tool box.

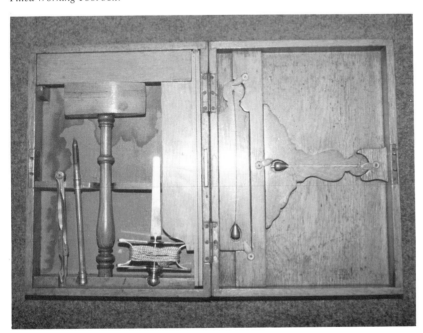

designs, gave 12in of space to describing the proposed hall and then later gave the bazaar a similar coverage.

The event was such as to affect even school attendances for the records of the St Martin's British School states: 'small attendances today on account of the Grand Masonic Procession and opening of the Bazaar.' The lodge members were indeed preceded by an excellent brass band and not only wore their aprons and collars but also carried some of their lodge emblems and implements. The idea almost baffles belief in the present day but not only were the brethren proud of their lodge and its contents but the public could rest assured that this was no insidious 'secret' body in their midst.

One remaining item of those days is a single account book which listed the charges involved in erecting this new town building. The wages book ran from 1 October 1870 to 8 March 1872 with a tell-tale gap in the winter of 1870, as the weather was then probably too bad for labour, and the total incurred here was £560. The operative masons employed received 3/4d to 3/8d a day whilst the rough labourers were given 2/- to 2/2d a day. The person overseeing this whole operation and signing the 'wages paid' accounts was Joseph Gibbon who was the Borough Surveyor and Manager of the Gas Works, but also a joining member of Cambrian Lodge in 1869. What is clear from this particular record is that all the materials required for the construction were clearly dealt with and paid for separately and it is thus revealing to read one solitary lodge minute for 5 April 1871 which says: 'that Bro White be authorised to procure Bath stone of the quality known as the "Coombe Down" for the columns of the new Masonic Hall'. The lodge was not just speculative in this case.

Kelly's Directory for the town in 1884 tells us that 'The Masonic Hall was consecrated and opened in 1872 and it was built at a cost of about £2,000. It consists of a great Hall with ante-room and entrance hall on the first floor, and a lodge room with ante-room on the second floor; the basement is occupied by a Banqueting room with offices. The hall is used for concerts and lectures and will hold about 600 persons . . .'

It is only when one considers what the present cost of erecting such a hall would be today that the full magnitude of the task undertaken by those few masons of a century ago can be appreciated. By great personal effort and not a little sacrifice, by the public and family interest aroused, by wise investment and sensibly calculated mortgages and not least by proper stewardship of the construction process itself a final figure of £1,942 was reached by the time it was thought proper to complete the work. On 29 September 1873 the site itself was conveyed, with the buildings thereon, to three Cambrian brethren for £100 and in 1903 the whole enterprise became at last the total and sole responsibility of the then appointed Trustees.

Meanwhile the hall had to be formally accepted, opened and dedicated. The lodge minutes for 13 June 1872 give us a clear account of what took place:

> 'The Lodge was opened in due form with solemn prayer. Provincial Grand Lodge then entered the Lodge Room and the ceremony of Consecration commenced, at the close of which the Brethren attended Divine Service in St Mary's Church, after which they returned to the Masonic Hall and the lodge was closed in due form with solemn prayer. In the evening a Banquet took place at the Mariners' Hotel'.

The report in the Herald newspaper added some very interesting further details. A large number of brethren from adjoining towns were present and the procession was composed of more than a 100 persons, 'wearing the *well known regalia* (author's italics) and decorations of the Craft'. The sermon at the church

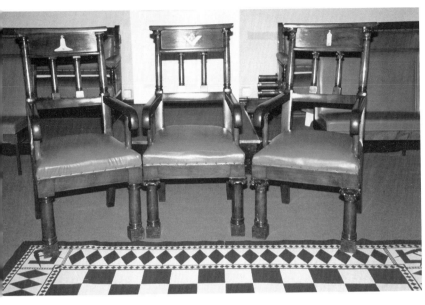

Principal Officers' chairs showing Doric influence in the legs and backs.

was preached by the Rev Latimer Jones of Carmarthen, whilst the organiser of the excellent catering at the hotel later was someone appropriately called Lamb. Some 80 people were then present and a donation was made to the Pembrokeshire and Haverfordwest Infirmary. It is a long tradition, we may note, that outside agencies have received masonic support.

From the moment that the new hall was occupied the brethren and Trustees began to both provide for it and show their appreciation of such a home. In July 1872 the Trustees fixed the price for letting the main hall — one night, 30/-; 2 nights, 2 guineas; for every night beyond the two, 10/- but all exclusive of the gas used. Lectures and Public Meetings were to be charged at 1 guinea and the Hallkeeper was paid 2/6d per night. There was to be a complaint about the 'gas' used by the brass band on practice nights but this soon subsided when it was made clear that it would all be paid for.

In 1874 J. Goldman presented a handsome lodge banner and this was augmented by John James when he became the W. Master of Cambrian Lodge in 1881 and gave another new banner for lodge use. In 1887 the large hall was the scene of a huge banquet as the lodge celebrated Queen Victoria's Jubilee, and the Installation dinners when the 4th and 6th Lord Kensingtons became Provincial Grand Masters showed again the benefit of having such a place for masons to gather. In 1898 T. James presented the lodge with a rough and perfect ashlar which had been fashioned in the quarries at Jerusalem. Today they have an honoured place in the lodge room beneath a glass domed case.

By 1903 there was a new urge to try and extend the masonic temple facilities but the Trustees were eager to pay off the remaining mortage first and thus only spent £150 on certain modest developments, as well as improving ventilation and introducing 'incandescent light' into the lodge room and large hall. Indeed, owing to the intervention of World War 1, it was not until 1924 that the main hall incorporated the previous stage, re-styled a new stage in the Regency Room below it, and installed some central heating. A photograph of this period shows the exterior with boundary walls and railings, and an iron gate at the top of the central steps to the main glass doors. These railings had not been part of the original plan and were removed during World War 2. The photograph also shows that between the central columns there was then suspended a pentacle or five-pointed star made of gas piping which was lit up on special occasions but this was also removed subsequently and now appears at the apex of the southern gable.

The alterations and improvements in 1924 were to some extent necessary, due to the use to which the hall and the lodge room had been put by the 5th Battalion Welch Regiment. The temple was actually employed first as a Sergeants' Mess and then later as a Corporals' retiring room and billets. Something of the same disruption occured in the second World War when the whole place became a reception centre for Continental and British refugees followed by its use as a recreation centre for American and Dutch troops. It was in 1954 that, after its derequisition, the old balcony overlooking the main hall was enclosed and made a most useful addition to the then otherwise cramped space of the previous temple. In 1970 this was further improved and the seating altered so that now some 90 people can gather there in comfort with space for more on special occasions.

Certainly the visitor to the Masonic Hall here today cannot but be impressed by the frontage which faces him as he enters the High Street that leads eventually to the castle at its steep upper end. Standing on a bank of five original wide stone steps are three pairs of 27ft high Corinthian pillars which in turn support a triangular pediment of ancient Greek form. Along a wall recessed behind this impressive portico are the tall glass doorway and five window embrasures that indicate the foyer and lodge room that lie within.

The downstairs foyer to which one immediately gains access is roomy without being spacious and is almost rectangular though with a steep flight of stairs rising to the right. Before 1961 this area incorporated a committee room which was also where the tyler prepared the candidates. 'From time to time', says the booklet prepared for the centenary of the hall in 1972, 'he would use the poker to stir the coals in the fireplace and his ostentatious concern over its temperature had a marked effect on the composure of the candidates or so 'tis said.' Today this is the area where visitors gather to await their summons to enter the lodge room upstairs when the more private and particular business of the lodges here — for there is a Cleddau as well as a Cambrian Lodge today — have been completed. The huge hall branching off from this foyer to the rear is now let out, as it has been for the last 120 years, to public tenants for their use — currently and most often a group that provides a 'disco' outlet for the locality. The lease provides protection from such tenants using the hall on lodge nights.

Passing up the stairs which remind one of the Second Degree we come to the ante-room where the present day tyler relaxes in a more centrally warmed atmosphere and checks that the register is signed and candidates are made ready when all have entered the lodge room. This latter is entered from the end of what is in effect a landing and it comprises the nearer upper area of the main hall that lies beneath. This is made all the more obvious by the covered alcove in what is the 'South' of the temple, behind the Junior Warden's chair, where rows of seats are placed under a lower ceiling, supported by slender metal pillars. This is the old balcony area of the main hall that has been transformed into part of the temple.

The actual temple is not unduly distinctive. The three chairs of the principal officers are obviously original and bear the distinctive symbols at their head whilst behind the Master's place stand the banners of Cambrian and Cleddau, at least when each lodge is meeting there. We know that the three tracing boards that used to hang on the wall and are now exposed on a separate central stand for each appropriate degree were placed there almost a century ago and the two kneeling stools, in the west and at the Master's pedestal, together with the large brass 'G', were presented by the Wardens of the day in 1918 as a thanksgiving for safe return to their masonic 'home'. Speaking of the main officers it is proper to note that the Master's jewel is hallmarked 1810, the Senior Warden's 1865 and the Junior Warden's 1900. The Immediate Past Master has a jewel that reverts to the very year in which this lodge of Cambrian began. The Master's and IPM's collars are both distinctive as having chains of office.

Neatly fitted into the west end of the old balcony recess there was first the new organ purchased in 1960 for £295, a sum which included not only the instrument but also its removal here and its fixing. It doubtless added to the appearance of this modest temple but it has been twice replaced and certainly, as with so many Welsh lodge meetings, a good instrument is a lodge requirement that is more than usually important as music still figures regularly in each degree ceremony. A framed warrant in manuscript signed by Zetland, Grand Master, and an intriguing frontispiece to the year book for 1923/4 when this hall was again restored to a proper shape and use, are other simple but distinctive features that give one a sense of this lodge's West Wales ancestry.

In 1972 the Cambrian Lodge organised the centenary of this meeting place by almost exactly copying the events of its inauguration though without a procession and Town Band. A service in St Mary's church was held followed by a meeting in the lodge room and a banquet in the main hall to follow. In 1989 the Cambrian Lodge has celebrated its own 150th anniversary and recalled with pride how it has seen here 2 Provincial Grand Masters as initiates and three members as Deputies. Though this meeting place may not boast in its internal appointments many of the fine possessions that adorn others in this volume yet the nature of its creation, its being part of the very fabric of the local society that masons are to strive to uphold and serve, and its continuity as the first specially appointed and designed masonic hall in this Province, are all sufficient reasons to make those who maintain or visit Haverfordwest's Hall aware of a real heritage. Its maintenance may be heavy to bear but its preservation is much to be hoped for. Here is a slice of Pembrokeshire past that it would be sad to part with.

Interior looking over Secretary's Table towards Master's Pedestal.

LLANELLI

(LLANELLI)

The Hall of a Prince and two Saints

A TRAVELLER PASSING through Llanelli in 1796 saw a very different place from the 'Town of St Elli' with which people have been familiar for the last 125 years. He wrote:

> 'Llanelly (sic) is a small town of 51 houses and governed by a Portreeve. The Parish is 7 miles long from Kaslwchwr to Pontyberem, and about 3 miles broad from the Lliedi River to Llannon.'

Small and unimportant as the town might then appear it had already been noticed by Queen Elizabeth I in 1566. In that year she appointed John Vaughan as the local Commissioner for the suppression of Piracy and it is on 2 April of that year that we have the first known reference to a coal shipment. The sailing vessel 'Le Saviour de Bydyford' carrying 2½ weys then set off for its Devon destination. From this small beginning the importance of Llanelli as a port developed and by 1856 there were 2,000 small sailing ships using the port each year and the coal export had reached 350,000 tons.

By that date also the seaside area of the town showed clear signs of its growing fortunes. Captains' and pilots' residences, shipbrokers', shipbuilders' and ropemakers' yards were established and there were also chain and anchor forges, ship chandlers and other longshoremen to add to the nautical scene. Moreover the sheer size of the old parish meant that advantage could be taken of the mineral resources that had been uncovered. There was the Copperworks begun in 1805; 26 collieries provided employment for 800 men; and the Dafen and Morfa tinworks, as well as the Lead works, all begun from 1841. With a Gasworks, a Pottery, a cotton and a woollen mill, not to mention a brewery, Llanelli was becoming a fair sized metropolis.

Although many of the present day features of the town — the Atheneum, the Market, All Saints Church and Stepney Street — had not yet been built it was only a few years before they were and the extension of the Great Western Railway to Carmarthen meant that links with that centre and Swansea were now much easier than hitherto. With these new possibilities of contact and a population that had trebled (to about 12,000) in the last decade, not to mention the broad increase in professions and trades, it is hardly surprising that 1856 was the year in which Llanelli saw the consecration of its first masonic lodge.

Residing in the town at this point were brethren belonging to lodges in Carmarthen and Swansea, Pembroke Dock and Brecon, Dundalk and Waterford. With the greater availability of help from the neighbouring larger towns it seemed at last possible to consider such a step as forming a new lodge and with a Civil Engineer, an Iron Founder and the proprietor of the Thomas Arms Hotel all waiting to be initiated it must surely have seemed more than a step in the dark. For the record, and to show how successful in terms of numbers the lodge was proved to be, seventeen meetings were held in the first year and fifteen new members were initiated, passed and raised.

Llanelli Masonic Hall.

F. Bolingbroke Ribbans, a Past Master of St Peter's Lodge, Carmarthen, the Worshipful Master of the Brecon Lodge in 1855, and the first PZ of the Merlin Chapter, undertook to become the Charter Master and such was his diligence that despite being Headmaster of the National Free School he attended all the regular meetings in his year *and* three of the six emergency ones, initiated 14 of the new brethren, passed ten and also raised them. It is hardly surprising that when he installed his successor in May 1857 he was presented with a piece of domestic plate and a signed address on vellum. He had certainly given Llanelli Freemasonry a remarkable start and set a standard for other Masters to follow.

With the introduction of John Eynon, Postmaster and proprietor of the Thomas Arms, into the lodge it was natural that this new 'Prince of Wales Lodge' should use that as their meeting place. By June 1856 the lodge had purchased seven Jewels, the tools and collars from Mr Evans of Great Queen Street, London, so that their meetings could appear with more decorum and regularity, and in February 1857 it was resolved that Eynon should henceforth be paid half-a-crown (12½p) for the use of the room in future, that one pound be paid for the previous provision of both fire and candles, and that at regular meetings bread and cheese and two glasses of 'good ale' would be provided. It was evident that the lodge was 'settling down' in its first home.

Yet in 1858 it was decided to build a separate masonic hall and on 5 July the Prince of Wales Lodge met for the last time at the Thomas Arms. Though the brethren met at the new hall in August it was to be 4 January 1859 before the premises could be officially inaugurated by the new Provincial Grand Master, RW Bro John Johnnes. It has to be said that the brethren had not moved very far for the new venue was a hall in the Old Road close by the hotel. Moreover it was not a place wholly at their disposal as half the ground floor which they used was partitioned off for use by those playing on the billiard table there. Later in 1859 they had moved again — and this time to an upper floor which could be properly tyled and kept for their use alone. This hall was eventually sold to the Oddfellows for £300.

No change in the location of Freemasonry in the growing town took place however for another 65 years. In that period the Lodge of St Elli had been consecrated (in July 1919) and there was already a Royal Arch Chapter, St Elliw, which had been begun in 1875. Already there were signs that a still further local lodge would be appreciated and it was thus that a general meeting of freemasons was called at the Old Hall on 23 June 1924. Representatives were appointed from the three masonic bodies meeting there and their task was to 'prepare a scheme for the erection of a new Masonic Temple, or the acquisition of a building suitable for conversion to a Temple'. The proposition was carried unanimously and a committee formed to begin the task. One of their first recommendations was that lodge dues be increased so that from an annual subscription of 3 guineas an amount of £1 11s 6d might be set aside for the necessary Building Fund.

An especially useful and leading member of the committee was Col W. Bramwell Jones, a local solicitor, and Commanding Officer of the local companies of the 4th Battn, the Welsh Regt TA. It was to be expected that he would have particular opportunities for knowing what properties might be the most suitable and available in the town. Indeed within twelve months it was reported that the Trustees of the Greenfield House Committee were making a *free* offer of a site for the erection of the proposed masonic hall. Their only condition, that the site was for a masonic temple only — and therefore presumably no club facilities — seemed ideal but the committee properly deferred a decision until proper inspection and plans had been provided and the fact that no more is heard of that proposal suggests that the report on the site was not satisfactory.

An alternative way forward seemed to present itself when the Llanelli Masonic Council was informed on 30 July 1926 that a property known as No 39, Thomas Street, had been acquired for the sum of £1,250 of which the Prince of Wales Lodge had guaranteed £1,100. Considering that the Masonic Council now had two further component members in the St Elli Lodge (consecrated in 1919) and the St Teilo Lodge (consecrated in 1925) it was all the more imperative that a meeting place of adequate size and facilities should be provided. However, any hopes of an early settlement of the issue were doomed to disappointment for there were legal problems over the nature of the body that should undertake the development of this property and it was not until 1929 that the Masonic Council could usefully meet again. When it did no real progress was made and at last in 1931 a letter had to be issued to all the local brethren pointing out that the Thomas Street building, despite some interim work done on it to protect and maintain it, was not suitable for the purpose for which it had been intended.

By 1934 an architect, Harold T. M. Griffiths, was appointed by the local lodges to carry out a survey of possible options elsewhere and W. Bramwell Jones now became the Chairman of the Council. At the very same meeting as his appointment was approved W. E. Clement reported that 'a plot of land in Harries Avenue, measuring approximately 80ft by 140ft, and at present let to a firm of contractors, was available and could be purchased for £500.' This time

The temple room looking east.

the Chairman allowed no further delay to occur and on 7 August 1935 he announced that the Thomas Street premises had been sold for £1,000 and that they had acquired the site in Harries Avenue for £565.

Things now moved on apace and after resolving that the new building would not be stone-faced but constructed in brick, an acceptable plan and elevation was drawn up together with a description of the interior and exterior of the whole hall. By 21 August it was announced that a tender by Mr Isaac Jones to build the hall for £1,500 was approved, and the foundation stone was laid shortly after by Harold Barker and D. G. Hogg. The long and protracted process which had begun twelve years before was at last happily concluded when, with proper masonic ceremonial, the RWor the Rt Hon Lord Kensington, Provincial Grand Master, carried out the dedication on 15 September 1936. The Provincial Grand Master was no doubt both impressed and encouraged by what he saw.

Today the contrast between the rush and bustle of traffic in the nearby town centre and the quiet surroundings of this masonic hall must be even more evident than when it was first erected. Though it is only 50 years ago the mere speed and volume of the passing cars and trucks, the motor bikes and vans is such that just to turn off into this side road and approach the site of the hall is an evident relaxation. Moreover it was foresight of the first order that arranged for the hall to be built where those coming in their cars could park and leave them with no stress whatever. There is ample space for even the largest numbers

The pillars placed at the entrance to the temple room at Llanelli.

likely to gather here and the 140ft of depth is obviously made use of on the busiest evenings.

Though lofty and broadly proportioned the outside of the hall makes no attempt to impress by its design or decoration. It is manifestly a commodious meeting place and must have satisfied the men in 1935 that here at last was a hall that was able to meet the needs of their many members. The fact that two further craft lodges (Unity and Trevor Kelway), a Mark Lodge and meetings for Knights Templar, Rose Croix, Royal and Select Masters and a further Royal Arch Chapter have all in turn required accommodation since its erection has been easily met and they in turn have made the upkeep of such a building more of a possibility so far.

Certainly there is no sense of cheese-paring in the furnishings and appointments within. The stained glass windows that greet one in the porchway or entrance to the Temple, and which can be seen to best advantage on turning to the light from inside, do not suggest that there is simply a bare hall without any sense of graciousness. Moreover the symbols which the windows bear clearly declare the hall's purpose and also remind the visitor of the teachings which he will receive within. The entrance hall, with its panelled walls and broad passageway, beckons one as if entering a modest manor house and allows easy access to the various rooms and foyer around it.

To the left and right of this entrance way are the Past Masters' Room in which are pictures of Grand Officers over the years, and a general room for Master Masons, committees or private conversation. Here, as one has been glad to notice in so many of the halls in Wales, are bookcases with a fine array of study material, including encyclopaedias, lodge minute books, a full set of *AQC* volumes, local lodge histories and the Provincial Year Books. The better known commentaries on the ritual are also here and the occasional works of lesser known authors dealing with little known corners of masonic history. The collections here are well housed and, one hopes, equally well used for there is much that could make the many aspects of Freemasonry practised here so much more enjoyable as their background and significance are better understood.

At the end of the hallway, with its rooms that were once used by a caretaker now providing kitchen and toilet facilities, there is a pleasant foyer or vestibule before one enters the porch to the main temple at the rear. The two pillars that stand sentinel outside the doorway were, like the same objects in Exeter, once placed inside the temple. However it was felt that they would be better preserved by being placed outside, at the entrance, as were the original pillars of the Temple at Jerusalem. Only one of the pillars has at present an actual globe. This is of some antiquity and it would no doubt be a matter of some interest to the local brethren to learn both the origin and the value of this original sphere.

On entering the temple one is struck by the mat that greets an entrant. 'C R O E S O', it declares, 'W E L C O M E' in the native language of Wales and it is fitting that in the temple beyond there has been a demonstration of the First Degree by a visiting lodge using the heavenly language of this land and a similar presentation of the Second Degree is shortly anticipated. Indeed the word 'rhagorol' (excellent, admirable) is surely the right one for the room into which we now pass. It is a room that fully accounts for the substantial dimensions of the building which we could observe from outside. The room is lofty and lengthy and the volume of it must add immeasurably to the dignity of the ceremonies that take place here. The ceiling with its rich colouring and, like the older hall at Carmarthen, with its own form of recessed lantern, enhances the delicate shades of the lower walls and leads one's eyes to the dignified east end where the Master's place, set in a simple archway, and with its fine array of Past Masters' chairs, completes the vista from the doorway.

The chairs of the three principal officers, as well as the chairs encircling the lodge, are all part of the original lodge furnishings and are excellent examples of the best of mid-Victorian handicraft. They each bear their appropriate emblems at the head and have very distinctive backs with plain shafts ending in a gentle arch. Seeing the Senior Warden's chair set against the banner of the Lliedi Mark Lodge is especially striking.

Yet this hall has other features. Passing out of the temple we can better observe the domed ceiling that pours light down upon the vestibule. We can also appreciate the well arranged boards recording the names of Past Masters of the five Llanelli Craft Lodges which accompany us to the foot of the winding

staircase. This wide stairway, with its fine iron scrollwork, leads us to the upper landing where we are faced with a row of glass doors opening on to what can only be described as a 'baronial' dining room. It may well have been designed for ladies nights as well as masonic dinners for there is quite enough space for dancing here, whilst the service lift that transports the food in the serving hatches from the kitchens below is arranged away from the room itself and over the area of the downstairs entrance hall. With its many windows, its ample lighting for night-time and its spaciousness this must have been a great adjunct to the social side of Freemasonry in the last half century. One is informed that it is indeed one of the great benefits of this building.

Here then, in this busy town that like so many other places hereabouts is having to adapt its industry and its outlook to a new century, we have a masonic hall that can adequately cope with the present and even some future growth in local Freemasonry. Those who for so long must have urged the creation of a better home for the Craft than was at first devised, and they included some of the most notable members of local society, would be quietly satisfied with the eventual outcome of their labours. Mr Isaac Jones, who carried these wishes into reality, was never a member of the Order though his son, the late Sidney Jones, was able to enjoy the hall which his father had created. He, like others since, must rejoice that so much understanding and imagination was exercised in providing this hall that Llanelli brethren will no doubt long appreciate.

The chairs of the principal officers.

MERTHYR TYDFIL

(MERTHYR TUDFIL)

The Hall in the Valleys

22 SEPTEMBER 1910 was both a memorable and a most important day in the life of the freemasons then meeting in Merthyr Tydfil. It was the occasion for celebrating their lodge's centenary, a meeting of Provincial Grand Lodge (South Wales, Eastern Division), a service at Cyfarthfa Church and, by no means least, the laying of the foundation stone of the new and present masonic hall in Pontmorlais, the upper end of the town. 'The day', we are told, 'was beautifully fine and no fewer than 300 brethren, representing lodges both in the British Empire and foreign climes, gathered together, and assisted to make the occasion a memorable one. The procession through the streets was one of the most imposing spectacles ever witnessed in the town, for it is very rarely, and only on special occasions, that Freemasons appear in public wearing their regalia and jewels.' (*Express office brochure.*)

The lodge premises in the lower High Street which were being used up to that time can be clearly distinguished to the present day for they have distinctive characteristics upon their façade. Yet the accommodation which they offered, and which today constitutes the Conservative Club, was quite inadequate for such an occasion as the one envisaged and so the committee took over the local Drill Hall which was able to provide one area for the lodge proceedings and a still bigger one for the banquet to follow. The invitation to luncheon was extended by Col. J J. Jones, Worshipful Master of the Loyal Cambrian Lodge, following the Provincial Grand Lodge meeting and the brethren then assembled outside the Drill Hall to walk to Christ Church, Cyfarthfa.

The route to the church was through High Street, Victoria Street, Penry Street, and up Aberdare Road to the church and the whole way was lined with admiring spectators who were fascinated by the aprons, chains, collars, and decorations worn by the passing brethren. It is not least to be remembered that they would see two tylers with drawn swords, bearers of corn, wine and oil, the banner of the Provincial Grand Lodge, a Chaplain with a bible on a cushion and the architect with his plans. At the church, and when the brethren were seated, the church was opened to the public and was soon 'crammed to the doors, many persons failing to get even standing room.' (*Brochure.*)

Amongst the Provincial Chaplains taking part was the Vicar of Troedyrhiw, whilst the address was given by the RW Past Provincial Grand Master of Herefordshire, The Very Rev the Hon J. W. Leigh, DD, Dean of Hereford. The service was the normal one of Evensong and during the last hymn a collection was taken for masonic charities in which others happily took part. The sermon had included the following observation: 'The object of Freemasonry was not only the erection of buildings but it was calculated to make men better and holier, and that was also the object of our Christianity, and so Freemasonry had been called the handmaiden to Christianity.' (*op cit* p4).

The procession then re-formed and passed through Bethesda Street and Vulcan Road to Park Place, opposite 'Tregenna', where the new masonic hall was to be erected. The Mayor and Mayoress (Councillor and Mrs F. T. James)

A major feature of the hall at Merthyr Tydfil are the two pillars in the temple. These are 150 years old and in excellent condition.

were in attendance for the ceremony of foundation stone laying and appear to have taken much interest in the whole proceeding. The building of which this was the first step was to be set up on the high ground facing Pontmorlais Circus and was carried out by Mr John Jenkins, the builder, according to the designs and plans of Charles Morgan Davies, a local architect. Davies was not only a member of Loyal Cambrian but also of the Ashlar Lodge of Mark Master Masons, of Tredegar, a member of the David Rees Lewis Royal Arch Chapter and a founder of the St Tydfil Lodge of MM Masons in Merthyr. He therefore well knew the purposes for which he was designing this building. It will also be of some interest to note that the Provincial Chaplain on this occasion was the Rev Peter Williams.

The actual completion and occupancy of this intended structure was not to be until January 1912 and before we come to that important event and the tour of the hall that could then be made it will be as well to look back a little and see how it was that a better set of premises for Masonry in Merthyr came to be required. We can best start this review by looking at the much valued and framed Charter of the Loyal Cambrian Lodge, No 110, which is carefully preserved in the present temple.

The fascinating thing about this document is that it bears the names of 'ATHOLE, Grand Master; M. Gillies, Senior Grand Warden, Thomas Harpur, Deputy Grand Master, and Thomas Mahon, Junior Grand Warden', who authorise the brethren, William Williams, William Edwards and William Williams, to act as rulers of their lodge from 1810, but also has a note:

'This warrant is registered in the Grand Lodge vol 6, Letter F. June *1768*.'

The Master's chair is made from Spanish mahogany and dates from 1834 whilst the canopy was presented to the lodge in 1912.

The reason for this apparent difference is only clear when it is recalled that Antients' lodges, of which this was one, were only allowed to come into existence if they could obtain a warrant of some lodge that had previously been authorised but which had now ceased to function. That was precisely the case here. The Warrant was registered as No 144 and this had been issued to a lodge that began meeting in the King's Head, the Strand, London, from 1766, but which had been subsequently cancelled in 1775. A petition for this then vacant charter was made by several brethren of the old Caerphilly Lodge No 126, who were all residents in Merthyr and who had been initiated between April 1808 and July 1810. As a result of a favourable reply to their application the new lodge was constituted on 7 August 1810 when the Worshipful Master of the Caerphilly Lodge duly formed the new unit and installed its first Master, all in the name of the Prince John, Duke of Atholl, Grand Master. Hence the new *form* of the Charter that Loyal Cambrian Lodge holds to this day.

At first this lodge met in the Castle Inn but in 1827 it removed to the Bush Hotel. On 2 June 1831 it is recorded that the lodge was not held that night owing to the disturbed state of the town when 'a tumultuous assembly . . . paraded the place and committed several outrages.' (*op cit.*) Loyal Cambrian brethren have a fascinating relic of that time of riots for the tyler's sword is one that was taken from a member of the Swansea Yeomanry on that occasion and has been handed down to its use here to this day. This item was joined by a crystal goblet, or Loving Cup, presented by Edward Lewis Richards, sometime County Court Judge for North Wales, in 1842, whilst in 1844 the two pillars, still retained, with their globes, were purchased for the lodge's use and presented by Dr Allday.

The arrival of the new chapter in the town and the growth of numbers in the lodge meant that by the 1860s there was an increasing desire to have a separate and private lodge room and one that was not attached to a licensed house. A report was presented in 1870 underlining these points and urging action but it was not to be until 1880 that active steps were taken to implement those recommendations. Several influential brethren, the foremost being Col D. R. Lewis, formed a public company which would provide not only a lodge room as hitherto but anterooms which would serve other essential purposes. The foundation stone for this venture was laid by the Deputy Provincial Grand Master on 6 September that year. It was not to prove the right solution.

With considerable foresight and application Thomas Wake, as an officer of the lodge and thus well aware of the obvious inadequacy of the High Street accommodation, made two suggestions as to how their difficulties might be overcome and one of these was to endeavour to form a company to build shops and lodge premises in the Pontmorlais Circus area. Only the failure to get the co-operation of the nearby shopholders prevented this scheme from being developed but it is interesting to note that the eventual and more lasting solution was to be in this very vicinity.

It was, as we have already noted, the advent of the Centenary year which seems to have concentrated the minds and wills of the Loyal Cambrian Lodge brethren so as to attempt some resolution of an increasing problem. The site to be obtained was only available from a Bro Major Morgan of Brecon in 1909. It was vested in a board of trustees so that what was erected on it would be devoted for ever to Freemasonry and so that it would be the absolute property of the lodge. When it came to the official opening of the new hall in 1912 it was again the Deputy Provincial Grand Master, WBro Tennant, who officiated as the Prov. Grand Master, Lord Llangattock, was now too unwell to attend. Both the front door of the building and the door of the temple upstairs were opened with golden keys and the brethren of Loyal Cambrian were congratulated on possessing such a beautiful edifice.

The brethren of Merthyr had and still have today a hall of which they can be properly proud. Erected at a cost of £2,800 the accommodation on the ground floor is ample and agreeable. It is reached from the pavement outside – in its own very pleasant and quiet cul-de-sac – by a short flight of steps beneath an imposing and dignified stone entrance porch. Indeed the façade of the building confirms that great care was taken to construct this hall with prime materials which have since mellowed and produced a sense of modest grandeur. The whole elevation is of local stone, coursed rock work up to the first level with the best red Beaufort facing bricks above that, with blue York stone dressings to the windows, doors, cornices, piers, columns and pediments. One senses that especial care was taken by Charles Davies, MSA, to complete each detail with loving care. The elevation facing across to Pontmorlais, with its lofty situation, is also built up of piers, cornices and pediments of the Doric order, so that though this is the rear of the building its appearance from below is worthy of its occupants.

Within there is the same sense of solid Edwardian workmanship. From the start the building was to be heated with gas radiators, and the dados are in panelled teak wood, whilst even the spacious dining room to the left of the entrance is well supplied with large and impressive fireplaces. There was to be no repetition here of the cramped and poor facilities of the earlier hall. There is a lounge, hall, cloak room, kitchen and several lavatory areas. The Merthyr brethren must at last have felt that they were inhabiting a worthwhile home from home. There is even an area today where the stewards might have their meal before the rest of the brethren come to dine, for here the masonic stewards are working officers at table in a very real sense.

It is time, however, to mount the stairs to the right of the entrance doors and ascend to the pleasant landing that now opens up before our view. There is again the same sense of warmth and solid decoration and no less care in having provided all the areas required for an easy approach to labour. Most striking to the eye are two distinctive items of Merthyr. One is an old floorcloth which has been most carefully preserved and displayed on the wall which on its further side forms the west end of the temple. It is unique in that it can serve as an aid for both the 1st and 2nd degrees and also shows the items which may seem familiar in quite different positions. It also shows the 'key' (or tongue of good report) which now rarely appears on masonic tracings.

Turning from this special exhibit we can see a fine stained glass window referring to St Tydfil, whose name is retained in that of the town. This gives another dimension of colour and quality to the landing whilst also fitting naturally with the somewhat ecclesiastical woodwork. At this end of the landing there is yet another toilet and a good preparation room close by the entrance to the temple proper. At the other end of the landing is a lounge which provides space for a library, pictures of Past Masters, and some useful store spaces.

As might be expected, however, it is the main temple itself which contains so much of significance in the increasingly long history of Loyal Cambrian Lodge, even if this hall is now used by much younger lodges also. It can only be their privilege to gather amongst so much of both aesthetic and historical value.

As we have seen in several other halls the eye is at once captured by the two great pillars and the kneeling stool between them. Already they are almost 150 years old and yet they seem to have been a fixture here for at least that long. With their globes attached they form a fitting feature to anyone's introduction to Masonry and one might occasionally regret that a new candidate does not have the chance to see the striking setting in which he is placed on first being admitted to such a lodge room.

Before these pillars and the centre of the floor is the 'new' case and tracing boards presented to Loyal Cambrian by D. R. Lewis in 1893, again almost a century ago. Until this presentation was made the lodge used its still preserved older boards which merit careful scrutiny. One, bearing the inscription 'Lodge No 144' (as it was in 1810) has features that associate it with the Holy Royal Arch though its open Volume of the Sacred Law showing 1 Kings, the two great pillars, again with globes, the square and compasses and the implement on the front of the pedestal all seem to suggest a Past Master's degree as much as anything else. Perhaps the fact that these are pre-Union Atholl emblems may imply that only such brethren were, in any case, fit candidates for the further step of the Holy Royal Arch. The lodge also has a reversible 2nd and 3rd degree board of about 1856 which in itself suggests their use when space for storage in an inn was at a premium.

Our eye will now be naturally drawn forwards and upwards to the fine Spanish mahogany chair and pedestal made by a Bro Jenkins in 1834. The former cost £3 10s 0d and the latter £5 10s 0d (£3.50 and £5.50 today). The matching candlestick, as with those at the Wardens' places, is of 1810 vintage. The chairs that flank that of the Master are also uniform and add to the sense of completeness in the arrangements in the east, though it is the old banners of Loyal Cambrian Lodge and the striking canopy above the Master's place that finally complete the picture. Of the latter we read on a small plaque, 'This Canopy was presented by Wor Bro & Ex Companion Jas Fraser PPGReg, as a tribute to the memory of Wor Bro & Ex Companion David Rees Lewis, PPGDC. February 1912.' Fraser was the Master in 1907 and this was clearly a gift to the lodge to mark the change of venue as well as the service of the freemason after whom the local chapter is named.

It was James Fraser who also made the ballot box numbered 1/2 and presented it to the lodge and chapter in December 1902. This was to take its place alongside the old ballot box (of 1810) that is still extant and which bears the number 144. Both these items sit on the secretary's desk before the old fireplace and present mantelpiece in the north. In his turn James Fraser, this generous benefactor to the lodge, is remembered by the present organ which was donated by the brethren as a token of respect to him.

Another benefactor who is much revered and properly recalled is Thomas Nibloe, a successful draper and cinema owner in the locality who gave the lodge its present chairs for the Wardens. He obviously had a new location in mind when these were given in 1907 and it is delightful to see how these later gifts match with the pedestals which were made by Evan Davies, a cabinet maker, in 1849. The Wardens' places are given their sense of age and continuity by having mallets from 1810, candlesticks from the same year and even their columns that graced the original meetings in the Bush Hotel.

'In addition to the old furniture, and working tools, the whole of which are in excellent preservation and in constant use, there is a set of eight Officers' old collars and jewels, which are of a unique design and of considerable value. The jewels are of sterling silver, and have been in regular use in the lodge since 1810,

Below: *The crystal loving cup of Loyal Cambrian Lodge dates from 1842.*

Below right: *The stained glass window that has been preserved and which refers to St Tydfil.*

and are still in perfect condition. They were manufactured by Thomas Harper, Jeweller, Strand, London, in 1809. Thomas Harper was Deputy Grand Master of the Ancient or Athole Grand Lodge from 1801-1813. He visited the Loyal Cambrian Lodge in 1812. The Officers' collars are probably of a design peculiar to a few of the old Athole lodges. The Ancients had no regulations for uniformity of clothing or jewels, consequently lodges had free choice in these matters. In many lodges the collar jewels were worn suspended by a narrow ribbon. The old collars were used by the officers of the Loyal Cambrian Lodge from 1810 to 6 April 1893. They were then replaced by collars as authorised by United Grand Lodge . . . (They) are preseved in a handsome mahogany case, presented to the lodge by the late Bro D. R. Lewis in 1893.' (*History of Loyal Cambrian Lodge*).

The case is now placed on the wall above the Junior Warden's seat and recalls the case of similar collars already mentioned during our visit to the Abergavenny hall.

Standing again in the west and surveying this fine room with its moulded piers, arches and cornices and its coved, panelled and enriched ceiling in plaster one can easily imagine the sense of pride and accomplishment that must have seized those brethren of 1912 when at last they took charge of their latest and still lasting masonic home. Here is a building to grace the town, to serve the Craft and give delight to those who have the privilege of visiting it. Certainly the newest members of the lodges that meet here can consider themselves fortunate that this is the 'birthplace' of their Masonry and anyone who longs to preserve the best of the past must give thanks that Loyal Cambrian Lodge has been so careful to retain its tangible links with its predecessors.

Gazing once more upon the detail of the Master's place and canopy, the picture of Rees Lewis, the lions couchants on the arms of the chair, the scroll and feathers and the rams' heads on the pillars at the sides, one rejoices at such care for a place of masonic meeting. Once again this hall reminds the masonic student of the wealth of history that we possess and the magnificent heritage that is ours. It is a heritage that Merthyr Tydfil stoutly supports.

The display of Thomas Harper 'Antient' jewels.

MILFORD HAVEN

(ABERDAUGLEDDAU)

Harbourside meeting place

ANYONE WHO MAKES the journey to Naples and Milford Haven will discover that their masonic halls have at least one feature in common. From their upstairs windows you may look out upon a wide inlet from the sea and recollect that in days past those waterways have given berth to some of England's most famous sailors and ships. Nelson, in particular, was associated with both ports and none who spends any appreciable time in either place can avoid the references to him that are still extant. It is, for instance, significant that the oldest lodge still meeting at the hall in Milford Haven, St David's, No 366, after starting at the Milford and Waterford Coffee House, Hakin, in 1821, moved within three years to the Lord Nelson Hotel on Hamilton Terrace.

The combination of these latter names is not fortuitous. The port owes its origin to Charles Greville, nephew of Sir William Hamilton, when he established it as a working harbour in 1793. The development of the local facilities for shipping was much more vigorously pursued after Nelson visited the area in 1802, during the period of his temporary retirement from active service following the Copenhagen campaign. Most biographies of the great admiral usually refer to this period as having been spent in quiet pursuits with the Hamiltons at Merton in Surrey, but there were excursions to other parts and one of them was undoubtedly a visit with Emma Hamilton to this part of Wales. She persuaded Nelson to recommend Milford as a repair base for HM Ships.

It was doubtless the impetus to local activity and a growth in the population that led in 1821 to the formation of Milford's first lodge, and even though the small Naval Dockyard had already been closed in 1814 there was still much shipping employment and the presence of the Irish Steam Packet Service. An early and exceptional event in the life of the lodge reveals that Milford was far from being a forgotten place.

On 13 September 1821, only months after the warrant of the lodge had been granted, an Emergency meeting was called for 4am (sic) 'for the purpose of receiving our Beloved Patron, King George IV'. It is good to know that masonic principles regarding the 'sovereign of one's native land' were so faithfully adhered to and the confirmation that the members of the lodge did in fact so fulfil their bounden duty and service is proved by the fact that four days later they were given permission to change the title of their lodge by adding the words '. . . or Loyal Lodge of King George IV'. It was a signal honour for a lodge on the most western extremity of the Principality.

The continuing and precious reminder of that early start to an honourable history is found to this day in the presence, at the north east corner of the present lodge room, of an ancient Master's chair. For many years it was used for that purpose when Old Priory Lodge was warranted in 1921 the Wor Masters presented a new chair and it was rightly decided to prevent anyone sitting in it so that it could continue to represent 'one of the most glorious examples ever recalled in the annals of local masonry'. The chair was presented by a Lewis Roper Fitzmaurice and bears on one of its back struts the words 'St David's

Milford Haven Masonic Hall overlooking the harbour.

Lodge', the date 1821, and a golden Welsh harp with the crown above. Nor is this all. Surmounting the chair, and supported by the two slender pillars that form the frame, is an arc of wood, painted gold and blue with inverted crenellation, and at its centre, in the place of a keystone, a blue panel bearing the inscription in gold 'G^{iv}R'. This panel is then also surmounted by a carved crown in gold, red and blue. Simple and stark as the rest of the chair may be we have here a most unusual item for any lodge and one that is properly regarded with pride and respect by the members of St David's or Loyal Lodge today.

The fortunes of Milford continued to improve and the docks were steadily extended and used throughout the century until in 1888 the work on them was completed. Other building work was also in progress for a new masonic hall was being constructed and the ceremony of taking over the new building took place in the autumn of 1882. Providing the funds for this work was not easy and as in the case of Haverfordwest earlier musical concerts, bazaars, choir evenings and other fund-raising events had to be held to ensure that the hall could be retained. It was not until 1906 that a Milford Haven Masonic Hall Co Ltd.

Incorporated was established so that the lodge members became Directors and shareholders. It was this year also that the freehold was purchased for £30 and in due course the other bodies that were to be formed here would take their share of the capital allocation. These include Kensington Chapter, Old Priory Lodge, St Bride's Mark Lodge and St Bride's Chapter of the Ancient and Accepted Rite. All these had been formed by 1923.

By this date the town had further developed for by 1914 2,000 local people were employed in the fishing industry and well over 200 'smacks' were to be found with an anchorage in the harbour. It is no surprise therefore that Freemasonry, like so many other activities, flourished and the possession of this hall was a real boon to the brethren of the locality. Nor is it to be doubted that a mark of the importance of the Craft hereabouts both then and since is shown by the fact that two of the Provincial Grand Masters, Lord Kensington from 1912 to 1937, and Col Kelway from 1945 to 1981, were members of St David's Lodge and the former was also an initiate there.

This fact is brought home to us at once on our entry into the premises. Having turned our back on the waters of the Haven across the main road we mount the seven steps that take us up to the recessed front door under the almost domestic style façade that abuts the pavement. Though the whole plot belongs to the freemasons yet the major part of the ground floor has been let out to a tenant and hence the working area of the masonic hall is on the first floor.

A pair of flights takes us to the landing which is tastefully decorated in white walls below and a pale blue above. Most of the wall facing the newcomer is covered with two display cases which between them contain the personal standard and masonic regalia of Rt Wor Bro Colonel the Rt Hon the Lord Kensington, CMG, DSO, once Provincial Grand Master of South Wales (Western Division). These mementoes of a very distinguished son of the lodge were presented by Lord Kensington's son, Wor Bro Lt Col the Hon Michael G. Edwardes, MBE, in September 1957. The gift was on behalf of the family and it is very good to see that the fine banner of this distinguished brother is retained in so pristine a condition a generation or more after its being so presented. No less would Lord Kensington have rejoiced to know that his son was also to be a most honoured freemason and to become the Grand Secretary of the Grand Lodge of Mark Master Masons as well as the holder of other comparable offices in the degrees associated with that position.

In the second of the cases there is, in addition to the regalia, a much used copy of the VSL and a somewhat time-soiled card that emphasises the continuing loyalty of the masonic brethren associated with this place. It is printed in pale blue, with the St David's Lodge crest at its head, and beneath an all-seeing eye in its radiant glory there comes a crowned and winged figure driving six horses with the names — England, America, Japan, France, Belgium and Italy — attached to their bridles. Around the figure are the words 'Victory to Peace' and beneath the hooves of the oncoming steeds are the further words, 'Welcome Home to Returned Brethren'. The card also bears the name of Vaughan Thomas and the date Friday, 12 December 1919. Simple as the card may be it is one of very few that record what, to the men who were spared that conflict's great demands of life, must have seemed a much valued thought as they came again to this masonic hall that they had for long had to forsake. It is such items that remind us of how masons have done their duty in all ages and it is singular that 1821 and 1919 are both marked in Milford Haven as times when brethren served their monarch.

To the right of the landing are the small committee or preparation room and the entrance to the commodious dining room with its view over the

neighbouring harbour. The room is lofty and not only seats many brethren but also has an ample bar space in one corner. The heavily curtained, tall casement window and the carpeted floor give a cosy look to the room and its acoustics are easy and helpful. It forms a fitting contrast to the temple that we enter next.

This is reached at the far end of the landing and runs at right angles to the former dining room. As you enter it you cannot but be struck by the two marble-style pillars that stand permanently at the west end of the central chequered carpet. The double-stepped bases of the pillars are apparently black marble with the shaft above of a tawny brown. Above these circular shafts we have the identical, yellowing chapiters with their two rows of pomegranate seeds, a formalised form of netting between them whilst below the rows there are symbolic lotus leaves interspersed with what look like ears of corn. Above the chapiters and on their own circular brown bases are two spheres of the terrestrial and celestial regions. With a richly woven blue-covered kneeling stool between them and a fine dark oak tracing board chest placed on the carpet before them this centrepiece of the lodge rivets your attention and focuses the rest of the room's pleasures.

One is now aware that like the bases of the pillars the whole room at ground level is formed of almost black panelling and seating. The only relief to this mass of dark colour is the rich red carpet that surrounds the central strip and the lighter mahogany chairs for the Master and his Wardens. Whilst the pedestals before these chairs are of a very dark brown shade albeit with a garter blue ornament of St David's Lodge on their face, the chairs are startlingly bright. They are very substantial, decorated with 'ecclesiastical-type' Gothic designs, both behind and beneath their blue cushioned seats, but with finely carved square, plumb and level in the triangular headpieces that complete each seat. The Master's chair, the work of WBro. Tom Newling, has two further adornments. A small bishop's mitre at its peak and two miniature pillars, complete with globes, rising from the sidepieces of the back frame and thus setting off the corbelled triangle of the headpiece. Placed, as has been said, amongst the dark furniture around and against the dark lower panels of the walls the chairs need no embellishment.

Yet it would be quite wrong to leave any impression of drabness or sombre quality in this room. Above this lower band of blackened furnishing the walls burst into a succession of cream panels bordered in rich red frames, whilst above the central carpet there is a most delightful four-sided sloping and recessed 'lantern' with the panels there coloured light blue but with white and red borders. From the midst of that lantern there hangs the inevitable 'G'.

Around the walls are a number of portraits of past Provincial Grand Masters and other local masons of note, as well as the warrants and certificates of the lodges and other bodies that now meet here. Amongst these of course is the proudly displayed centenary warrant of St David's or Loyal George IV Lodge though already that lodge can begin to look with confidence to the day when this warrant will be joined by its bi-centenary partner. The pictures are well chosen and it is good nowadays to note that whilst we still recall in our lodges the tokens of the past we have left behind those days when every inch of such a lodge room would be covered with dusty frames.

The priceless 1821 chair to the right of the Master has already been described but there are other items in this room that deserve our attention. One of these is the very pleasant set of officers' chairs that were provided from the outset of 1821. At first sight these may appear to be a quite ordinary set of plain upright dining chairs with dark brown backs, legs and bases but on more careful scrutiny

Dining Chair with Officer's badge carved on back part of a set.

one notes that the backs are carefully designed, with common square pillars and small spheres framing the backs, four trefoils piercing the rear frames, and between them a lozenge with a circle and then, in each circle, the appropriate emblem for the officer concerned. Only in the case of the Secretary and Treasurer is the emblem painted in lighter wood at the tops of their backs. These chairs thus add a real touch of antiquity and order to the whole room as well as marking for each occupant a reminder of their 'progress through life'.

The lists of Past Masters and Principals in this room are all affixed to the east end of the temple and in the cream wall spaces already referred to. The gold lettering on blue or crimson backgrounds creates a real sense of quality and illumination on what might otherwise be a rather bare area and yet the room is not overburdened with the more substantial kind of boards that are often seen.

Finally, passing from the east and noting afresh the coffered and moulded cornices of the ceiling, one's eyes are led to the north west corner of the room where, in a slight recess, beyond the line of the central pillars, we see a most fitting and pleasant organ console, with its enveloping pipe case. This was installed in 1947 and was dedicated at another joint meeting of St David's and the Old Priory Lodge on 6 May that year. The organ was purchased with money that had been subscribed by members of both lodges and the dedication was performed by the Provincial Grand Chaplain, the Rev P. G. Wallis, who was later to become Deputy Provincial Grand Master. The care of this instrument is such that it looks as if it had been but recently obtained and yet it is already approaching its jubilee. For lodges such as we shall meet here, where the singing of hymns is part of the normal ceremonies that are conducted, an instrument

Right: *King George IV Chair.*

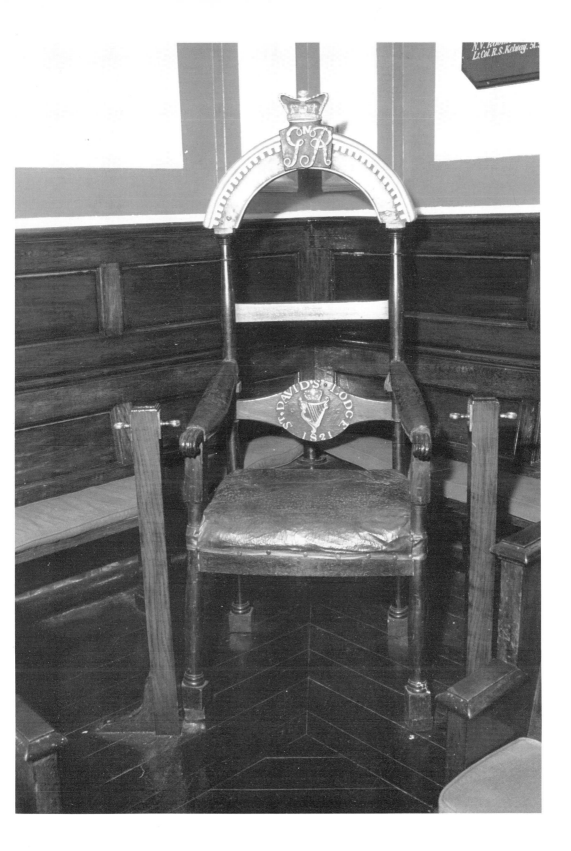

such as this is a particular boon. As a piece of furniture it gladdens the eye of a visitor and those who know about such things declare that it has a most pleasing tone.

It is on such a note that we may now take our leave of yet another of the halls in this part of West Wales. Whilst the once flourishing fishing fleet is reduced to but a score of boats and the Irish Steam Packet Company long ago moved its operational base to Pembroke Dock yet the modern world, with its constant need for oil and petrol products, has seen new jobs and professions created in these parts. It is men from the refineries and shipping berths attached to them that serve this new kind of industry and already form part of the membership of both St David's and Old Priory. Modern as their occupations may be they boast no less a pride in the history of their lodge and its hall's past. For those who are but visitors and guests there are delights to savour here that we hope are now revealed. Combined with a warmth of welcome one can also make a daily advancement in masonic knowledge by calling at this hall with its view over the water.

'Welcome Home' Greeting Card to brethren returning from World War 1.

(TREFYNWY)

The Converted Wool House

THERE HAVE BEEN meeting places for masons in Monmouth for the last 220 years. As early as 1768 a lodge numbered 414 is recorded in Lane's Engraved List as being warranted in the January of that year though sadly it was to cease meeting by 1773. On 2 January 1815 we have evidence of the Royal Augustus Lodge No 656 though it was not in fact constituted until SUNDAY 22 April. This lodge met originally at the 'Crown and Thistle' Inn and in the temple of the present masonic hall there is a direct link with that original meeting place. It is the original door of the Royal Augustus Lodge room which is now doing service once more as the entrance to the organ loft above the Secretary's desk on the north wall. The door was fortunately saved when the property in which it had remained was pulled down in 1931 to enable the Woolworths store to be built. The previous owner, WBro W. E. Day, then kindly presented the door to the Loyal Monmouth Lodge which was the successor of the 'Royal Augustus'.

'The old door is a very fine piece of work but its appearance has been somewhat marred by having been painted. The upper panel is square and is filled in with a glazed circle containing two concentric rings about a central circle (or boss). Each of these two rings is divided into eight separate lights; the lights of the outer ring being mirrored glass and those of the inner ring being glazed with ruby-tinted glass. The central circle is a concave mirror. The stars in the inner circle covered peep-holes.' (*Freemasonry in Monmouthshire*).

To have such a link with this older lodge is all the more remarkable because on 16 June 1816 – again a SUNDAY – the Royal Augustus Lodge moved to the King's Head in Agincourt Square (a timely reminder of the link between Monmouth and Henry, Prince of Wales, later Henry V). There it remained until 1830 when it was also erased. This door therefore may be said to be in a double sense a means of entering into the past of Freemasonry in these parts – it links us with both a demolished site and a dissolved lodge. There was, however, another lodge locally when a dispensation was granted for a military lodge to be held in the Royal Monmouth Militia. Numbered 664 on the 1814 list the dispensation here was dated 10 July 1815. The life of this body was even shorter than the others just mentioned for Grand Lodge demanded the return of the warrant in 1816 and the lodge was in erased in 1822.

It was with some local talent in the Craft still around, however, that we see the warranting of the Loyal Monmouth Lodge as from 21 December 1838. It was constituted in January 1839 but a Bro Smith's house caught fire in 1840 so that today the lodge only possesses a warrant of confirmation dated 10 March 1841. Meeting first at the Bell Inn, Church Street, the lodge was able to take up residence in the present building from 1841. As they did so some of the members such as Farrow and Rees may either have remembered or read what happened in the Royal Augustus Lodge in 1816. In a letter written to the Secretary of the Vitruvian Lodge of Ross-on-Wye it stated: 'The Pillars of your lodge were sent per North's Wagon on Tuesday last, hope they arrived in time, I am desired to thank the Master and Brothers of the "Vitruvian" Lodge for the use of them.

Charles Smith, Sec.' It would appear that furnishings were often borrowed at that period and the newly settled Monmouth brethren may well have determined to set up their own once they had a hall that was theirs. One sees the results in the hall of today.

Passing south from the centre of the town towards Monk Street where the present Hall is situated one's eyes can easily be drawn to the rear of the property where a clearly displayed square and compasses on an upper, outer wall speaks of the house's purpose. We are in fact being directed to that very same late Regency building which was first leased by the same Loyal Monmouth Lodge as exists today. As we shall see the interior fully bears out the sense of 150 years of occupation that brethren here have enjoyed.

We know from the property deeds of this hall that in August 1846 there was a release of a timber yard, warehouse, or woolhouse, and cottages from a George V. Maddox, architect, to the Rev I. E. Tyler by way of mortgage and reconveyance. The recipient in this instance was very appropriately named for already the woolhouse, with a dwelling house and brewery close attached, had been rented to the local freemasons as their hall. In 1887 another document which authorised a succession of duty to Isabella Gertrude Elizabeth Jones, daugher of Mary Jones, widow of the Rev Thomas Jones, reveals that 'a building formerly a wool loft, converted into a Freemasons Hall, and four tenements adjoining and partly underneath, and a cottage near or adjoining with a small garden leading to the River Monnow were occupied as follows:

Freemasons . . . . . . £16 0s 0d per annum' and the other tenement dwellers' rents follow. (L. E. Hayward. *Loyal Monmouth Lodge history*)

It was not to be until 12 September 1911 that the title to the property was to be sold to the Loyal Monmouth Lodge as a result of the original will of the Rev Thomas Jones, Rector of Hempstead. At this stage Miss I. G. E. Jones sold her rights to the property for £550 and four trustees were appointed who then confirmed the letting of the four cottages, yard and roadway. Following the purchase of the property a good deal of repair and renovation took place with gas fires being installed to replace the open fires of which the fireplaces are still visible. The seating was replaced, the organ put in its present position and the entrance doors to the temple moved from the south west corner of the lodge room to the present position at the far end of the ante-room.

A fascinating picture still retained amongst the hall's archives shows the three-storeyed tenements that occupied part of the yard space which now provides a useful parking area. In that picture the hall's frontage is identical with what we find today, with a large G placed in the triangular pediment of white with a black border, three window spaces on the first floor (two of them blocked up) and two large 'Square and Compasses' in a band across the heads of the two small side doors and the large arched central door at ground level. This latter porchway, which is not now used, also has a gilt G above its door panels. The whole of the rest of the façade is white with black lines marking the band with the emblems. There are two windows on the left of the doorways and three on the right. The latter compose the cottage which is today occupied by a resident custodian and his wife.

It was in 1939 that the cottages in the yard were taken down, new gates and pillars erected at the road access, and further renovations to the building carried out. Following World War 2 a new roof was put on the building, the whole of the interior was redecorated, including the Temple, and the entrance became its present size. Finally the gas fires gave way to central heating, the lodge room was re-carpeted, a new chequered paving was purchased and the present pillars in the west were made. It is the temple as thus restored that we shall shortly be visiting but before we once more return there we should once again turn back to the lodge's history and then look at the ante-room.

What may well have decided the Loyal Monmouth Lodge to look for a more permanent home was the request made in January 1840 by Wilks, the innkeeper of the 'King's Head', that they should forego their lodge meeting as the room they normally used was needed for a Special Commission to try the Chartists who rioted at Newport. If this was to become more regular and it had happened in 1839 it was clear that difficulties of maintaining their progress would be in jeopardy and the lodge, after all, was only two years old. That the move to Monk Street stabilized the lodge seems undoubted and in September 1841 there was to be a joining member whose family would not only honour local Masonry but would be well represented in the portraits that today adorn those premises.

The brother concerned was Alexander Rolls, an initiate of Lowestoft Lodge No 84. He was duly passed and raised in 1842 and in December of that year was also ballotted for and accepted as Worshipful Master for the ensuing year. In the same year John Etherington Welch Rolls was also ballotted for and initiated and after a rather more deliberate progress to the chair (1848) he was to go on to become Provinical Grand Master of Monmouthshire from 1863-70. He was the father of John Allen Rolls who became Lord Llangattock, the PGM of South Wales, Eastern Division from 1894 (see Cardiff hall). A painting of Lord Llangattock in full regalia hangs in this temple in which he ruled as Master in 1864 and 1910. His father's picture is also framed beside the fireplace on the north wall.

Another matter of some interest in connection with the early life of Loyal Monmouth Lodge is that as from the time of its consecration there are listed an *Inner* Tyler as well as an *Outer* Tyler. They both seem to have been paid officers and must have been appointed in accordance with prevailing custom in these parts. Their presence would explain what even in other halls has sometimes been a mystery – why should there be *two* swords which are referred to as 'Tylers swords'. In the Windsor temple there are two such swords crossed over the entrance to the lodge room and even in the Newport library and museum there are displayed a tyler's sword and a paradise (or curvy) sword. The matter is one that might well provide material for local study and a short explanation for the advancement of brethen's knowledge. By 1841 however, doubtless as they came to Monk Street and had to pay more for their domestic expenses, there was a resolution 'That the duties of the paid inner guard be dispensed with and that in future the Junior mason present at any Lodge night shall perform that duty on that night.'

On entering the present masonic hall one is still very aware of the original working nature of the building in which masons now meet. The flagged floor, the plain walls and absence of furniture speak of simpler days and attention to the necessities of business whilst the long, low-ceilinged corridor that leads off to the right (albeit marked over its doorway with a fine white circular panel announcing the lodge's name and number) little prepares one for the well-appointed and abundant furnishings that are to come. Here, without any fuss, are pegs to hang coats and umbrellas and at the end of the corridor the usual offices. It is only when you turn right before the latter that the whole character of the hall begins to alter substantially. We are at last in Loyal Monmouth's private 'home'.

Right: *This temple used to store bales of wool until the building was sold to the local masons.*

Arrive in the daylight and you will at once be struck by the rural scene that greets you through the ante-room window. Here is the garden leading down to the Monnow that was referred to earlier. Here we are in the part of the building that on the outside proudly declares that freemasons meet within. You are at once in a comfortable Victorian room, with fine neo-Gothic carved cupboards beside the window, a soft carpet on the floor and pictures around the wall. Over the doorway into the temple is the oldest banner of the lodge and running from the doorway along the lower wall opposite the window there are glass cases that were fortuitously discovered at Goodrich Castle, costing only £5, and fitted here by WBro Hayward, the past Provincial Tyler and custodian. The cases are full of items of local and even more general masonic interest that have been accumulated from generation to generation. They stem from a resolution passed in this lodge in March 1890 when it was decided that 'a Library and Museum be established in connection with the Lodge. Bro Sevier, PM, presented the lodge with a very old firing glass, and Bro Oakley, PM, presented Gould's *History of Freemasonry* in three volumes'. A year later the custom of regularly giving *AQC* volumes was also begun. As we have seen in other Welsh halls so here there is ample attention to the materials for study and masonic education. It was the desire of our forefathers that these should be made available and now their efforts have amassed some items of real interest.

Here we shall find an old Master's cocked hat, the large hour glass that symbolised, if it did not measure, the passing of time, three charming ebony-headed and ivory-handled gavels marked for the lodge's use and a typical Victorian stand to hold the toast list or menu at the social board. Here too are the lectures presented in 1880 by Bros Thos H. Clarke 'on Mechanical Appliances, containing a photograph of the Triangles, Blocks, Winch, etc etc'. There is a fairly rare book by George Fort of 1876 entitled *The Early History and Antiquity of Freemasonry* whilst from almost a century later we have a book written by a local freemason, D. W. Peel, which tells the story of the roof garden at Barker's store at Kensington in 1960. The cases are worthy of anyone's attention and local brethren are indeed well served to have such a collection so thoughtfully looked after.

Above these cases there is a large heavily framed portrait. It is that of Isaac Chilcott who was one of the most noted members of the Loyal Monmouth Lodge as well as having been a former member of the Royal Augustus. After having been for many years head waiter at the 'Beaufort Arms' and thereafter a boarding house keeper, he served the lodge for several years as a steward, acted occasionally as a Warden and was finally Worshipful Master in 1842. Writing of him in 1843 in the *Freemasons' Quarterly Review* a reporter said:

> 'The Loyal Lodge, 671, until lately nearly defunct, has, through the industry and zeal of Isaac Chilcott, not only revived, but is actually in most excellent order, and rapidly increasing in number and respectability, thirteen having been initiated, and as many joining; among the latter, the High Sheriff. Bro Chilcott's zeal is most commendable; he attributes his success entirely to having read and studied to the best of his power, the masonic works of the Rev Dr Oliver.'

It is with such a character to greet one in this part of the building that we can properly enter the temple which he and his many new brethren in Loyal Monmouth must have begun to appreciate as their lodge grew in stature. It is a room of great character and filled with items of much interest and anyone who comes here for the first time may well find himself somewhat overawed by the variety of the contents. We cannot do better than begin by looking at the very striking decor.

The room itself is long and lofty and it was here that originally the bales of wool were stored. The original central doorway that we saw on the outside is now completely covered from view within the Regency style canopy and hanging red drapes that envelop the Master's place in the east. The top of this quasi-tent has a band of golden letters at its crown – on the left side 'AUDE VIDE TACE' and on the right 'SIT LUX'. One is immediately taken back to the days of William IV and the start of this present lodge but also the Royal Augustus that preceded it. Moreover the whole setting of this canopy is impressive.

Our eyes having been raised almost to the roof we may notice that the ceiling is of light fawn colour which in its turn contrasts with the red band that now surrounds the upper walls, and merges with the red curtaining of the Master's place. This in turn gives way to another lower band of light blue and that to a line of white followed by dark blue. One suddenly becomes aware that there, surrounding the whole temple, are the major colours of the curtains of the Holy of Holies and the very expression of the Royal Arch Chapter. Against this upper symbolism of rich decoration the still lighter blue surfaces at ground level show off the pictures, warrants, certificates and even the chairs and tables. As a dado

The door that was once used in the original meeting place now serves as an entrance to the organ loft.

around the top of these lower walls there is an alternative frieze of MM and RA Tau signs in gilt. The care obviously shown in so presenting the whole room with a colour plan is pleasant to observe and instructive to ponder. To have taken less care would easily have left this room gaunt and heavy.

The Master's chair is set on its usual three steps and is behind a large pedestal on which hang at the sides those large wooden level and plumb which no doubt play their part in the 3° ceremony. The candlestick itself is mounted on a set of three steps with all of them completely chequered, whilst the chair is a fine oak piece with rich blue upholstery at its back. Above the chair and under the canopy head is a roundel bearing a large 'square' with its arms pointing upwards, whilst below it, and partly covered by the chair is the large and original 3° board. The 2° and 1° boards are, not surprisingly, behind the Senior Warden's and Junior Warden's chairs respectively. Of the Master's chair it should be noted that it was presented in 1867 when the minutes state that a vote of thanks was accorded to Bro E. Bromage for his handsome gift 'in the shape of a very valuable chair for the M.'

Moving round the temple from the Master's place in a clockwise direction we may note another old banner of the lodge, this time of a very simple design but

Part of the fine collection of books and items of masonic interest at Monmouth hall.

much used, the black boards showing Past Masters, and the Red boards of the Past Principals, each set one side or other of the Junior Warden, and the intriguing little wickets that adorn both the Wardens' pedestals. In the south west corner, where the oldest entrance to the lodge room once was, there are now white painted organ pipes and these contrast sharply with the black globes that adorn the tops of the two great pillars at the western end of the chequered flooring. The pillars are some eight feet high with strong upright rectangular bases and fawn coloured shafts but each with the same type of decoration for their chapiters.

Above the organ pipes and against the dark blue walling we now see the first of several large portraits, this one being that of Lord Llangattock. To the right of the temple doorway and on the north wall there is a reputed picture of Prince Rupert whilst alongside him is one of George III. The presence of these items, along with the Provincial Grand Masters nearer to the east means that the room has a real sense of being lived in. Whereas the modern style is to remove pictures we have a vivid sense of being in a room long occupied by our brethren who must have gazed, as we do, on these figures of the past.

Meanwhile we must not overlook the organ loft that has both a recess and a projecting bay above the old door from the 'Crown and Thistle' as well as the secretary's desk. The decorative balustrade on the front of the loft also carries 2 crossed square and compasses and a pentagram whilst above the light blue wall behind the console is a broad arched panel in red with a large roundel and letter G at its centre. This feature breaks the otherwise double cube shape of the whole room and with its fitting contribution to the whole colour scheme makes its own rich variation between the accompanying pictures.

Beneath this balcony and flanking the old door we come to what are certainly some of the most remarkable items in this Hall. They are four Irish certificates, each bearing elaborate seals and having attractively coloured headings. To describe them in detail here might prove wearisome but for those who may wish to examine them more closely – and they deserve close attention by any advanced student of Masonry – it will be enough to indicate something of each heading and their greeting: From left to right they run:

(1) A bridge of four arches with an ark on the waters:
    'To the enlightened Knights of the Red Cross and Noachidaes to whom this shall come before – Greeting.
    In Hoc Signo Vinces.' ......

(2) An altar of seven candles with a priest, two men above an arch lowering a man down through the gap, a burning bush and a man with a snake:
    '*And God* said let there be *light* and there was *light* and the *light* shineth in Darkness and the Darkness comprehended it not.
    We the High Priests GGG of the Grand Chapter of an Excellent Superexcellent and Royal Arch Masons of Lodge (850) held in the town of Tullamore . . .'

(3) A cubic stone bearing the letters H $\overset{J}{V}$ H with a priest, an open grave with a bush growing out of it, a crucifix and two robed figures carrying between them the Ark.
    'Glory be to God on High *Peace* on Earth and to man good will.
    We the Chief High Priests and *Royal* Deacons of the most glorious and Magnanimous Order of Priesthood of the Union Band *according* to the Order of Melchesadeck . . .'

(4) a triangle with twelve burning candles above a coffin, a Calvary scene with a lamb, dove and cock below the cross, and two figures with one blowing a horn.

'In the name of the Most Holy Glorious and Undivided Trinity Father, Son and *Holy Ghost* Amen – Amen – Amen.

We the Captain General GGG of the General Encampment of Knights Templar and of Knights of Malta....'

It will be seen that how these certificates came to be in the possession of this lodge is itself a story worth discovering but even more revealing would be to know how it was that this lodge decided that these early 19th century items from over the water should have such a foremost place in the decoration and adornment of this ancient lodge room.

This is even more a mystery when we discover that up the winding stairs from the plain entrance hall we come to an upstairs room where there is another equally rare certificate. This one, also framed and with a pronounced geometric design, is headed 'This is to certify

T.I.T.E.A.P.F.O.L.W.R.S.A.P.'

and it bears the seals, on the left, of the S.W. Menatzchim, and on the right, R.W.M. Harodim. The figures of the seals are first St John the Baptist and then St John the Evangelist. It bears no exposed date. To those for whom the Order of the Harodim has for long proved a fascination this piece of unexpected evidence is of especial significance. It is but one more of the many treasures that this old hall has to reveal to its visitors and it certainly renders it unique. If to those who regularly frequent this hall their meeting place does indeed fill them with pride they may be assured that their feelings are fully justified. This is a hall that would justify any visit.

NEATH
(CASTELL-NEDD)

The Cambrian Experience

THE MASONIC HALL at Neath is certainly at the heart of things. Walk into the centre of this bustling little town and there, suddenly amongst the shops and businesses of a normal street, you will find the astonishing façade of the local masonic centre. It rises immediately, perpendicular, from the narrow pavement with its grey and yellow stonework rising some 35 to 40ft above you. It is in fact so high that it is with difficulty that you can grasp the whole effect even when you make your way through the parked cars and stand on the far side of the street.

Certainly the Cambrian Lodge masons who erected this hall in 1848 were quite unashamed of their presence in the town as the decoration of this façade makes clear. Unmistakable against the sombre stonework are two tall courses of white stone formed into two great pillars with decoration at their head which first suggests two gargoyles and can then be made out to be a simple form of Corinthian leaf and scroll work. Between the pillars is, at ground level, a symbolic doorway with white head and copestones and above it a recess, some 6ft higher, with a white roundel containing a carved square and compasses and a scroll displayed beneath. Parallel to the roundel's head and above it again is an arch with a prominent white keystone extended to the broad white band that crosses the whole façade at the level of the pillars' Corinthian chapiters.

Three such doorways, roundels, scrolls and arches in all appear, two of the sets on the outer sides of the two pillars, save that in the right hand set (as you face the building) the doorway is the actual entrance to the hall. Not surprisingly it has three shallow steps for those who come to a lodge here.

Yet even this is not all. The two roundels of the outer sets of features show the two globes that would normally rest on the heads of the pillars, one terrestrial and the other celestial. Moreover, above the pillars' heads and the white band that marks the actual roof line there is yet another broad course of masonry with antique courbel decoration, a slightly jutting parapet and a bold central feature of another roundel, this one displaying the 'all-seeing eye'. For what might otherwise be considered a quite modest if increasingly ancient lodge in a perfectly ordinary town this invitation to the visitor surely was and is both unexpected and telling.

The Cambrian Lodge which created this building was not the first lodge to meet in Neath. That distinction belonged to the 'Knoll (or Gnoll) Lodge' that took its name from Gnoll House or Castle built for a Thomas Evans in 1659. The lodge was founded in 1777 and worked at the Angel Inn there until 1784 when it transferred to the Ship and Castle Inn on the Parade (later to become the Castle Hotel). As a Derbyshire family, the Mackworths, married into the Evans inheritance through Thomas's granddaughter, Mary, they extended the house and increased their land holding to 12,000 acres. They were much involved in developing the local industries of coppersmelting and silver refining and Mary's husband, Sir Humphrey, is even recorded as fitting sails to the coal waggons so as to help the horses pull their loads more easily to the waiting ships. This

enterprising knight had a son who married into the Digby family and it was his grandson who became Lord of the Manor and owner of this large estate in 1765. His name was Herbert and besides being Portreeve of Neath, an MP, Colonel of the Militia and a Fellow of the Royal Society he was also made a mason in 1779 in Knoll Lodge, followed by his second son, Digby Mackworth. The link of this lodge with the locality was not just in a name.

After 1787 the lodge seems to have begun to change its character somewhat and by 1800 it was meeting in Swansea. Its future progress cannot occupy us here (see the chapter on Swansea) but it is to be noted that some of the artefacts of the Gnoll Lodge were retained by Neath masons even when it had begun its life elsewhere. The story of these items, most of which are still on view in the Neath Hall, is as follows.

Sir Herbert Mackworth died on the 25 October 1791. Not only had he become Master of Gnoll Lodge but he was in 1779 appointed Provincial Grand Master for South Wales, then an undivided unit. He died sadly at the quite early age of 54 in October 1791 due to a poisoned finger caused by a neglected thorn. His son, Sir Robert Humphrey Mackworth, died without issue in 1794 and it was thus Sir Robert's next brother, Sir Digby Mackworth, who inherited the estate. He had been Master of the lodge in 1788 and it was he who, again Master in 1799, agreed to the move of the lodge to Swansea.

Sir Digby presented a sword for the use of the Inner Guard and this sword, which is now in the care of the later Cambrian Lodge, bears a double inscription — the first reads: 'The gift of Digby Mackworth, Esq. To the Gnoll Lodge, No 412.' whilst the second is: 'Restored by Sir Arthur Mackworth, Bart, Feb, 1878'. Sir Arthur was also instrumental in restoring to Neath the old Gnoll banner which bore the name of Digby Mackworth as its donor. This latter was a fine piece carrying the donor's coat of arms with his name added on a scroll beneath, whilst above the arms was a crowing cock and another scroll with the words 'GWELL ANGAU NA CHYWILYDD' (Better death then shame). It is salutary for readers to note that this and nine other banners were thrown out as 'rags' when a heating engineer was working on the premises.

The Volume of the Sacred Law still used by the Cambrian Lodge at Installations or meetings of special importance carries the inscription, 'Gnoll Lodge, No 412, the gift of Brother Walter Williams, Junior Warden. 1788. Rees Jeffreys, Secretary.' and whilst this is an evident link between the candidates that come to make their obligations now and those of that period long ago there is also a tangible connection between the Junior Wardens of those long separated periods. Rees Jeffreys, at the first meeting of the Cambrian Lodge, was to hand over to it the furniture and jewels of the Gnoll Lodge though sadly only that of the Junior Warden remains intact. It is inscribed, 'Gnoll Lodge, 506, South Wales, AL 5783.' This dating is such that it also confirms the age of the jewel because it was obviously computed by subtracting 4,004 years to obtain the date, 1779. The same applies to a brass square which has also been retained from those beginnings and which bears the words, 'Gnoll Lodge, 412, South Wales, AL 5785'. It was only after the Union of the Grand Lodges that the difference between AL and AD was altered to 4,000 years only.

We have not, however, explained how it was that if the Gnoll Lodge left its native town there was any other masonic body to receive the items that were obviously regarded as the property of Neath Masonry rather than the possessions of the lodge that had started there . . . a concept that would not be easy for masons today to accept. The fact that these items were preserved and handed on eventually by brethren who might not have a local lodge but who had a sense of masonic continuity goes some way to explaining why there once more grew up a desire to have another lodge that could be more permanently established in the town of Neath. What certainly seems to have triggered off this idea as a possible reality was the visit of the Master, officers and brethren of the old Gnoll Lodge, now called the Indefatigable and Beaufort Lodge, for the purpose of laying the corner-stone of the Neath Town Hall on 31 May 1820. The Neath members of the Swansea Lodge, together with James Coke, the Portreeve of the town, arranged the ceremony according to the ancient rites and customs and not least with the approval of the builder, Thomas Bowen, who was also a member of the Craft. The Royal Arch and Knights Templar masons of Swansea were in attendance and their presence must have added noticeably to the public appearance of the brethren. As W. H. Jones says in his *History of Indefatigable Lodge, No 237*, 'The procession through the streets of the town of the masons fully clothed and bearing all the insignia of their several offices,

Looking east. Note the painted ceiling in the alcove with All Seeing Eye and on the left the unusual fireplace decoration.

together, we may be sure, with their modest and correct demeanour, brought out a desire for emulation, which no long time afterwards was advanced by an application to Grand Lodge for a new lodge.'

It was fitting therefore that the petition for this new unit in Neath should be recommended by the Swansea lodge and three months later, on 1 February 1821, the Cambrian Lodge first met at the White Hart Inn, Duck Street though it was not until 24 June 1823 that it was duly and regularly consecrated. Nine of the founders were already members of Indefatigable Lodge. For ten years it flourished, moving to the Eagle Inn, Wind Street, but after its further removal to the Castle Inn, where the Gnoll had met, it began to lose its vigour and only the efforts of a George E. Aubrey in 1844 led to what was a definite revival of the Cambrian members' interest. By 1848 the renewed desire of the Neath masons to have a hall of their own was at last rewarded and Tuesday, 6 June, was chosen as the day for opening their new meeting place. Members of Indefatigable were invited as guests and from that time to this the fraternal relations between the two lodges has been of the warmest.

It is interesting to note that as early as 1822 the lodge minutes record that an offer by H. E. Evans, of Eagle-bush, to purchase plans and designs for building a masonic hall was accepted but that no record then exists of any further action being taken. What had also happened in these intervening years was that the lodge had been acquiring some of the very distinctive items that were to grace the new hall when it was consecrated on 8 August 1848.

We have already noted that there were items from the Gnoll Lodge which were handed over for the use of the new Neath lodge but at that same meeting there is a minute that Mr Thos. Ashford of Swansea be employed to make the Banner, Tressel Board, Emblems, etc as well as a chair for the Worshipful Master. All these items are still in evidence in the present building and the Tressel (or Tracing) Board that hangs in the south west corner of the temple was repainted by Charles Saunders of Neath after the lodge's revival in 1843.

To the fine set of Thomas Harper jewels which were ordered in 1821 — a set which reveal some slight but interesting variations — there was added the first chaplain's jewel which today has its own case. This was purchased in 1845 for the Rev David Jeffreys, Rector of Neath and Prov. Grand Chaplain from 1848-52. The jewel was in fact found in some rubbish at the old Tram Depot in the town by a relative of a Past Master, Emrys Jenkins, of Swansea. He kindly forwarded it in 1941 to WBro. A. J. Lawson Taylor, a Past Master of the Cambrian Lodge.

The two great, though modest brown, pillars with their ringed globes that now stand on the extreme ends of the dais in the east of the temple had been bought in 1844 and for the Consecration all the collars and gauntlets had been specially repaired. To look round the present hall, therefore, is to be reminded of how diligently the brethren of the early years had prepared themselves for this great day of new dedication.

The structure behind the façade already described was built in 1847/48 by N. B. Allen and John Townsend, the contractor, to designs by Egbert Moxham, the architect. The events of the 'opening' on 6 June were fully reported in the local paper, the *Cambrian*, which also mentioned that this was so far the only hall specially devoted to the use of the Order in the Principality. The following week a Bro J. M. Buck, who was described as 'The Magician King', gave two special performances in the hall thus making these the first two public engagements to take place there.

The consecration of the hall in August also saw the Installation of E. J. Hutchings as the first Provincial Grand Master for the now separate Eastern

The view west shows the painted setting sun. The entrance to the temple is on the left beneath the organ loft.

Division of South Wales. Cambrian Lodge members were made officers in the new Province as Chaplain, Treasurer, Junior Gd Deacon, Organist & Tyler.

The hall as then designed was somewhat different to the one which we see today in that there was 'a neat little gallery attached to the Hall' where on some occasions, such as the Provincial Grand Lodge meeting of 1852, the ladies were admitted and seated. This gallery must have projected the width of the present recess at the west end and been reached by stairs leading from the adjoining entrance corridor on the north. There was then no organ loft and the Master's place must have been against the wall of the slightly curved alcove at the east end. We also know, from a letter written as late as 1921, of another feature that has long since disappeared. 'The retiring room was a very limited one beneath the gallery. There was no accommodation for retiring for refreshments, and it was customary at the close of the Lodge to set up in the body of the lodge a temporary table by the aid of tressels. Bread and cheese and beer constituted the fare, and the long clay pipes known as Churchwardens were strongly in evidence. Something warm by way of comfort followed, when the kettle was brought round by 'our jolly old Tyler' who provided himself with his snuff horn and sought all and each to have a pinch, usually favouring us with his favourite song, *The Laird of Cockpen*.' (Private letter from WBro W. G. Davies.)

Quaint as all this may seem it was only the next stage from the days when the lodge was opened and held around a dining table — with tressels — in the previous century, but it was not to the liking of increasingly sophisticated Victorian masons and in 1870 the gallery and its lower room were removed and alternative arrangements made, especially after the tyler and his wife moved into the house next door which the lodge had now built. It was at this time that the present dais was introduced at the east end and a Conclave of the Red Cross of Constantine and Knights of Rome (sic) asked permission to use the hall, thus adding some useful extra income. A warrant of this body still adorns the temple walls.

It was 1901 before the lodge committee could consider enlarging the premises by purchasing the large room of the British Schools at the rear of their plot, and also a small parcel of ground to the north. This at least allowed a new dining room to be built and a simple kitchen attached. This obviously encouraged still further efforts and in due time the whole of the present ante-rooms and facilities for refreshment, including the new upstairs dining hall, were added. It is thus time to look a little more carefully at the hall that lies behind that striking street front.

Entering by the three steps of the recessed porch we enter a narrow hallway with a most attractive Victorian lamp. Against the plain colour wash of the walls its golden coloured metal frame stands out all the more clearly and its adaptation to electric from gas light has in no way affected its usefulness or charm. Decorated on three of its six sides with the square and compasses it was obviously designed for this location and must have given as much delight to those early brethren as it can to a visitor today. In what could have been an otherwise drab entranceway it at once speaks of care and concern for the hall to which it leads the visitor.

From the hallway we pass into the sizeable ante-room with several exhibits on the walls, most of which have already been alluded to, and from here we turn

A Victorian lamp with masonic symbols.

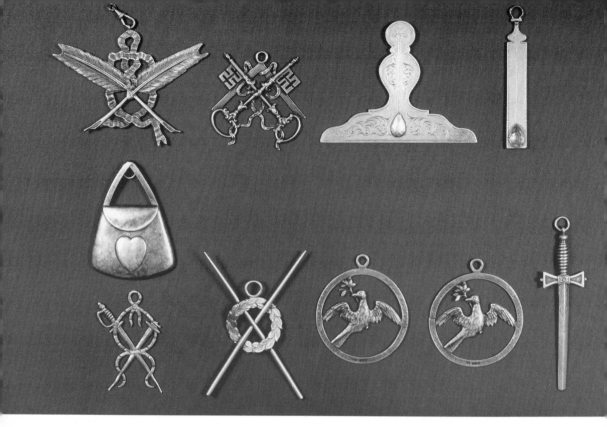

The set of Thomas Harper jewels date from 1821.

left again through the fine oak door that gives entry into the main temple. The warm panelling throughout gives both a sense of domesticity and richness to the whole and this is enhanced by the fine array of chairs that greets one in the east. The Master's chair dominates the rest with its similar, stepped but higher back and with two simple pillars and their tiny globes projecting from the extension above the headrest. This and the Past Masters' chairs flanking it are all well upholstered in red brocade and are of ample proportions.

Behind them is a fine curved seat that extends the whole width of the east end alcove, and above that hang the banners of the three lodges meeting here — Cambrian, Gnoll (a new one founded in 1928) and the Lodge of St Illtyd (1945). Higher still and above the broad white and gold cornice that separates panelling from ceiling, there is a shallow arch painted in an imitation stone colour and bearing the familiar words 'AUDI VIDE TACE' amongst a cluster of stars, as if in the firmament. Below this arch and filling the alcove roof gap is a large 'All-Seeing Eye' with the rays dispersing amongst the simulated clouds.

Matching the two pillars already referred to there are two lovely wooden chairs for the senior deacon and Director of Ceremonies, each with crossed legs and fine pierced backs. The whole effect is one of solidity and dignity and must be especially impressive for a new member receiving the charge.

Opposite the Junior Warden's place and behind the secretary's table with its own blue-silk covered table light there stands a most remarkable, ornamental fireplace. It consists of a great semi-circle of white stone pierced at the base with

Right: *The Tressel (Tracing) Board painted by Thomas Ashford of Swansea in the early 18th century.*

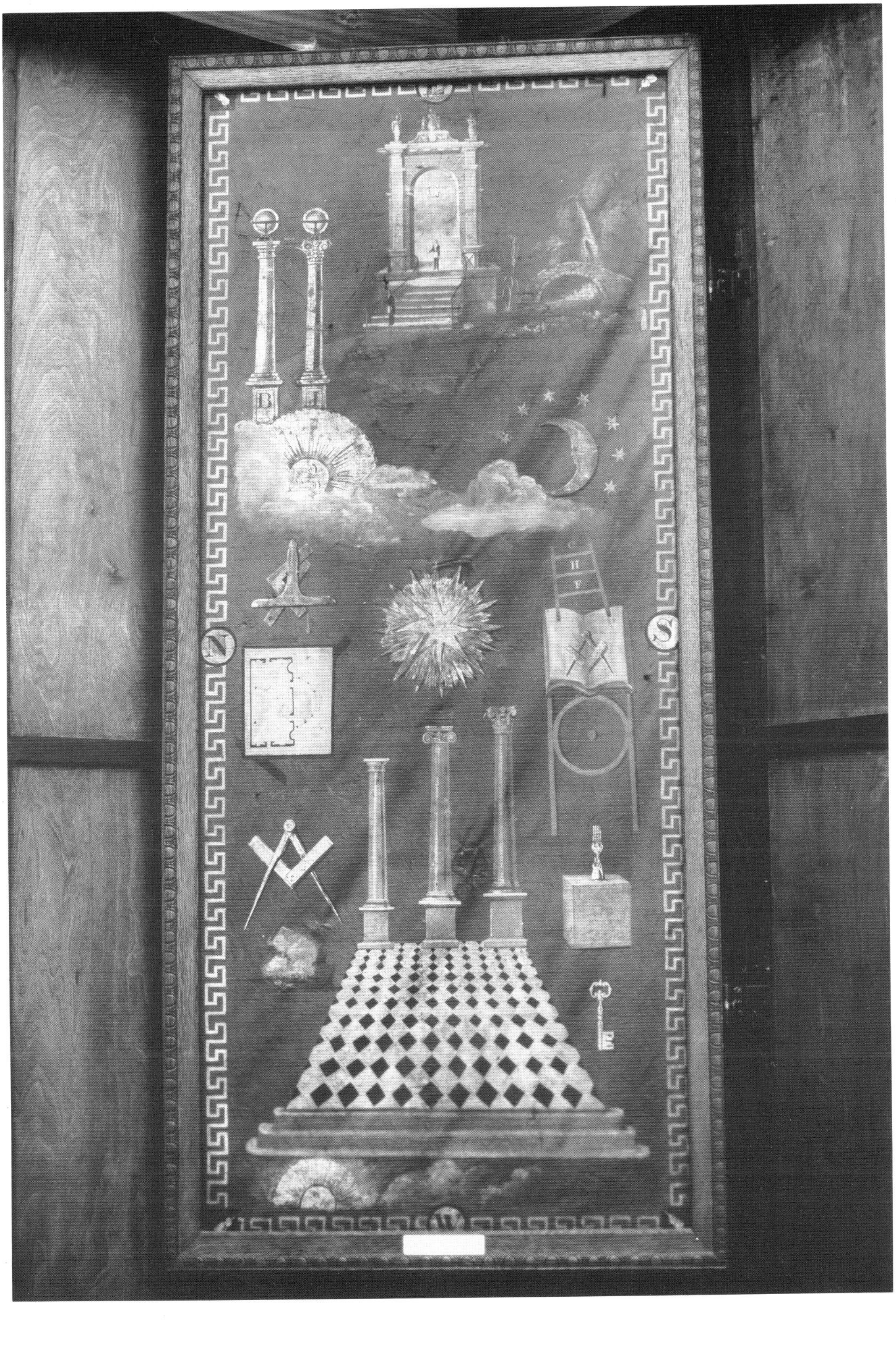
B
C
H
F
N
S
W

a recess where a fire would normally have been expected. Here there is a slab of Victorian multi-coloured tiling in front of which the bench for Secretary and Treasurer is placed. Above the recess is a symbolic mantlepiece and in the centre of this is set a blue-edged keystone bearing a gilt square and compasses. This is surmounted by a gilt-edged roundel with a letter G at its centre and this is still further crowned by a great semi-circle of blue stone bearing the golden rays of a sun. It seems a very proper sign to face the Junior Warden who represents that planet at midday. The whole feature dominates that north side of the room and strikes any visitor who enters.

Turning back towards the west one's eyes are drawn upwards to the representation of the blue sky with setting sun and the clouds flecked with the evening rays. This scene adorns the lower part of the ceiling across the whole width of the room and above the cornice as in the east. Beneath the white cornice with its blue and gold strip one notes the fine Past Masters' board of the Cambrian Lodge which was presented by the well known Deputy Provincial Grand Master, Edgar J. Rutter, in 1938. Alongside it in the south-west corner hangs the ancient 'tressel-board' to which we have already referred.

Last but by no means least in this lovely temple our attention may properly be drawn to the tasteful organ loft that now has its place above the entrance door. This seven-posted gallery front, the organ casing and the stairs leading up to it were in fact a gift by the brethren of the Indefatigable Lodge when they left their older home in Caer Street, Swansea to go to St Helen's Road. The incorporation of these features in this temple is a real work of art for the whole looks as if it had been there from the outset. It was not until 1929 that a committee was formed to consider the purchase of a new organ to complete this new addition to the room but their work was well done, the brethren produced the funds required and the late Bro E. H. L. Salter built and installed the console and pipes. The total effect is most satisfying and much appreciated in a lodge where music is still a very real part of masonic ritual practice.

This is indeed a hall of which the local users can be justly proud. The imposing façade does not fail to convey a sense of impressiveness within and Neath masons must be very glad that their forefathers of 150 years ago laid the foundations for later work so well.

(CASNEWYDD)

A Home for the Silurians

LOWER DOCK STREET hardly sounds like the most inviting address for a fine masonic hall. Yet those who take the trouble to visit this centre will not be disappointed. Once you have gained entry by the main door, on the curved corner of this rectangular site, you can feel time drop away from the twentieth century bustle outside and enter the early Victorian period when this hall was first opened for use. A sharp turn to the right takes you to the foot of a proper winding staircase that follows that curved wall outside and brings you up its stone treads with iron balustrade to a small landing. Alongside the stair and around the landing are niches with busts of local masonic figures, white against their pale blue background. These further reminders or the past also bring the place to life and recall the members of the Silurian Lodge who were responsible for providing this masonic centre. Three men in particular 'suffice to bridge the river of years between the first meeting of the Silurian Lodge and the celebration of its centenary — Samuel Coombs, the Founder Master; R. B. Evans, Master in 1864 and Secretary from 1872 till 1898; and A. Ernest Jones, initiated 5 March, 1890, Master in 1896.' (*History of the Silurian Lodge*. W. J. T. Collins. 1941. pp94f.)

This Samuel Coombs (or Combs as he is also recorded) is first mentioned as one of four visitors to an earlier Newport Lodge, the Royal Cambrian, that received an Antient or Atholl warrant in 1809. In 1815 Samual Combs became a member of Royal Cambrian and in view of his longstanding association with Freemasonry in this town it is hardly surprising that his portrait still hangs in this masonic hall today. He was still one of the Past Masters of Royal Cambrian when it was erased from the roll of Grand Lodge in 1830 and it is therefore a real link with the past when he is installed as the Charter Master of the new Silurian Lodge in 1840. We are given a further hint of the link in this hall when, turning off the small corridor that leads from the landing we enter the 'Tea Room', a charming apartment with a sideboard and dining table from which the early Silurians took refreshment when meeting in this part of the building. Moreover, above the sideboard is a masonic treasure, a pre-Union tracing cloth of individual design which presumably belonged to the older lodge and is now very correctly framed and preserved here. It will richly repay any local masonic student to examine its many features and seek to understand why they are placed on the cloth in this way.

When numbers warranted it the inner wall of this Tea Room could be folded back as it is merely made up of partitions. This then gave access to the adjoining room which today is the hall's museum and library but which was clearly the assembly room and supper room for larger gatherings of the Silurian Lodge. This is confirmed by the presence of a dumb waiter which could bring food from the kitchens below to this upper room that in its turn adjoins the original Temple. Even so the room is not overlarge and is rather long than wide though it has so many contents that perhaps its true dimensions are disguised. If the ancient tracing cloth in the Tea Room whetted the appetite of a masonic

Newport Masonic Hall.

historian then this room today is a veritable treasure house of masonic memorabilia. The real problem is to know where to start in describing it.

A case that stands alongside the dumb waiter has a full set of firing glasses. This in itself might not seem so unusual as many halls have such items but here the variation is that these glasses are made of what seems like venetian-style red glass and yet marked with the Silurian Lodge No 471. The grandfather clock case that stands alongside this display adds dignity and homeliness to the room and though not adorned, as are some such pieces in our masonic meeting places, with hour numbers composed of masonic emblems it suggests that the members of Silurian who dined here were not so engaged in their festive boards as to forget the time altogether.

On the wall opposite are three huge cases with glass fronts and occupying half the length of the room's wall on this side. There must be well over 50 items here of extreme interest to any student of the masonic past and in this case especially those who concentrate on the Holy Royal Arch. There are, for example, the original ensigns of the Silurian Chapter, made of metal and bearing very distinctive and differing emblems from the normal ones. A comparison with those listed and illustrated in Harry Mendoza's important book, *The Ensigns of the Tweve Tribes of Israel* would suggest that here there are yet further examples of local divergence and thus of particular importance for masonic knowledge as a whole.

Here too are rare and perfect examples of Aaron's Rod — the one showing it as a flowering branch, and the other as a serpent — which were almost certainly used in the now discontinued ceremony of the Veils that formed part of the original Chapter working. I find it to be intriguing that along with Coombs we have evidence that amongst visitors to Newport in the Royal Cambrian period were brethren from Bristol — and it is there today that we have, restored and preserved, the only normal working of the veils ceremony under the Supreme Grand Chapter of England.

Here too are preserved not only a complete set of Royal Arch headdresses for the three Principals but three parallel crowns that were placed at the chairs of the Principals and may well have continued to be used when the headdresses were discontinued in the early 19th century. For those specially interested there is even a special headdress here for the Sovereign of a Red Cross of Constantine and Rome conclave — a most unusual and rare item. Here too are a High Priest's breastplate with the jewels of the Urim and the Thummim together with an intriguing black bowl that is clearly marked as belonging to the 'Silurian' chapter. Most fascinating of all, however, are the three metal plates which are kept in this case. They are obviously home-made but they are also clearly of some antiquity. The first shows a large letter G with a triangular design around it; the second has an upright triangle which is surrounded by a cloudlike 'shekinah'; and the third is a simple triangle but with the point downwards. As alternative forms for the top of the altar or pedestal in the Holy Royal Arch ceremony they seem to have a place but exactly why they were all needed or whether they were changed during the ceremony does not seem to be known. The first of them certainly seems to confirm that an earlier age were content with very much what is proposed as normal usage today.

For the Knight Templar mason there are also reminders here of a time when possibly Royal Cambrian worked its own KT ceremonies or an earlier Encampment left behind its old symbols. Certainly the Knight Templar Preceptory once working here — Gwent No 115 — cannot have laid claim to them or it would seem that they could still be used though the Lamb, Cock and Dove are rather larger than those employed normally today. The old officers' tools employed by the Master and Wardens bring us back to the Craft though the remarkable and very ancient Maul with its rope that were unearthed in the Tura Escarpment in the vicinity of the Euphrates also remind us of the truly antique nature of the work which we now symbolize.

All too briefly does this list record the treasure house and its contents that just this part of the Newport Hall contains. When to all this varied collection of antique items one moves on to the fine collection of masonic books and pamphlets that are also kept here together with portraits and banners one is bound to confess that this must be one of Wales's most commendable masonic heritages. If this is merely taken for granted one suspects that in time it could be quite overlooked or even forgotten. Here is a rich mine for much future study and instruction.

Yet the visitor has another great treat in store. Turn back to the landing and pass this time through another door to the left. You are now entering the original Silurian temple that was first used after the building was dedicated in 1858. We have here a lavishly decorated early Victorian lodge room at its very best. Indeed the masonic traveller may feel, as in the museum alongside it, that he hardly knows where to begin in admiring the contents. He can do no better than turn round and lift up his eyes to the top of the entrance door through which he had just passed. Here he will find a rainbow arch enclosing the fully-coloured arms of the United Grand Lodge of England. Here in one item alone there is the sense of ancient and modern combined, not merely by the heraldic devices but also by the whole associated with the earliest Noachic period of British Freemasonry. One is reminded of the same style of entrance in

Barnstaple just across the Severn estuary (See *Masonic Halls of England — The South*).

Looking to the left along the west end of the room we note the very special Inner Guard's chair, the fine and imposing oak casing and pipes of the organ, with the Senior Warden's chair on its two steps before it, and on the far side the balancing door with, this time, the old banner of the Albert Edward Prince of Wales Lodge above it. Yet the west end of the temple would be incompletely described without mentioning the dark blue covered kneeling stool flanked by 2 tall white pillars on square bases, each side of the latter decorated with its own gilt square and compass design. Moreover these pillars are properly completed with 2 actual globes affixed to their chapiters. These are correctly drawn terrestrial and celestial spheres and the whole combination means that these items could take their place with the very best in England and Wales. The candidate must look or feel dominated by these pillars in what is a comparatively limited space and yet the impact of these two 'sentinels', if only because they do so fill the view and the area at the west, convey just the right impression of being both important and meaningful for the ceremonies of admission. One can well imagine that had this remained the only temple in the building someone might eventually have recommended that the pillars be placed elsewhere — even possibly outside the door (as at Llanelli) — but happily for our remembrance we have the arrangement still that Newport masons of nearly 140 years ago admired and accepted. Standing at that stool and looking east we can also the better experience their emotions.

Before the candidate would stand the large and well finished board case whose contents still have the dimensions that link them with the tracing cloth size in the Tea room. Painted for this lodge the boards have the general form that was recommended after the Union though with individual touches that show how personalised these productions could be. Few such boards, for instance, accurately reproduce the Hebrew characters that are asssociated with the middle chamber, and there are other varieties that have the Senior Warden inside or outside the chamber door and some that do not have him at all. These things do not finally matter but they make every board worth examining and ensure that each lodge of any age may well have tracing boards that carry their own distinctive format (for those wanting to see an especial case of this the ones at Weymouth are recommended: *Masonic Halls of England, — The South.*)

Above the tracing boards the lofty ceiling carries a beautifully decorated emblem of a large circle embracing a gilt Seal of Solomon — the interlaced triangles — enclosing a large letter G. The white expanse sets off this ancient form and links it with another such symbol, only this time with crossed square and compasses at the centre, in the middle of the Wor Master's chairback on its rostrum at the east. This rostrum is of three red carpeted steps before which stands the separate altar at their foot. The red carpet here is a continuation of the red papered walls of the whole room and it is against this rich, warm background that we encounter the almost overpowering canopy that surrounds the Master's place in the east.

This consists of two square columns rising from the level of the rostrum, ending in two huge and block-like chapiters that carry an equally large and recessed alcove roof which is shaped like the inside of a shell. The whole remarkable outer structure, so vast for this otherwise quite modest room is in white with gilt lines and edges, though the shell-like area is in pale blue with gold edging. Surmounting the canopy is a semicircular attachment displaying in gold on white the square and compasses in the 3° position.

The Silurian Temple at Newport. Of special interest is the impressive organ and the two pillars and globes. The tracing boards are in the centre.

It is within this white and gold frame that there stands a large early Victorian Master's chair. With a rich dark blue back covered by seven gilt stars and the emblem already referred to in the centre, dark blue cushion and almost black frame, arm rests and legs the chair completes the ensemble and takes its place naturally amongst the other array of blue upholstered armchairs that stretch to the wall on the right side of the Master's place. When put together as a whole the east and west ends, with the crimson walls and fine ceiling, make a room from the past that will be long remembered. It is, one imagines, even more impressive now than when it was first also fitted out with an array of heavily framed Victorian paintings.

This then forms the core of the building that was first begun with a laying of the foundation stone on 29 August 1855. It was the venture of the members of the Silurian Lodge alone even if the Provincial Grand Master might also have had hopes of this being the eventual centre of the whole Province. These brethren erected it in what was then the busiest part of town and their confidence was such and their foresight so wise that even when the needs of Masonry here overstretched the bounds of their first temple and dining areas they could expand without having to move. Part of the dispensation read on that great occasion is worth repeating as it sets such events in a context that we may regret having lost —

The Silurian Temple with the finely decorated east wall.

'Whereas it has been represented to me that you . . . are desirous of giving solemnity to the Ceremonial (of stone-laying) by a public procession to divine worship in St Paul's Church at Newport aforesaid, —

I, Charles John Kemeys-Tynte, Member of Parliament, Colonel of the Royal Glamorgan Light Infantry, PGM for all Monmouthshire, lawfully constituted, do hereby authorise you to . . . proceed in your masonic clothing and insignia to the above Church . . . and when the foundation stone shall have been duly levelled to return in like manner up Dock Road, Dock Street, Llanarth Street into Commercial Street to the said Town Hall . . . and that due order and decorum be preserved and the Honour of the Craft maintained.'

What may be of peculiar interest to the reader is to learn that in first addressing the local brethren on this day the PGM spoke to them as 'diligent workmen of our Secret Craft', and yet in the authorised procession that then took to the open street we read that the brethren following 'Six Union flags and Six Flags of all nations (?) borne by the Sons of Master Masons; there followed officers with their collars and lodge jewels, the rough and smooth ashlars, the Tracing Boards uncovered *and* the Mayor and Town Council of Newport! No less impressive but certainly more normal was the attendance of the Deputy PGM for Bristol, and the PGMs of Hereford, Oxford and also Australia.

This was not quite the end of the surprises in terms of present day practice for on reaching the church entrance a normal form of processional path was formed down which the PGM with his Sword Bearer passed first into the building with the band playing the National Anthem. On reaching the site of the stone-laying we are told that the proceedings began with these words — 'Men, Women and Children here assembled today to behold this Ceremony, — Know all of you that we be lawful Masons, true to the laws of our Country, and established of old with peace and honour in most countries, to do good to our Brethren, to build great Buildings, and to fear God Who is the Great Architect of all things. We have among us, concealed from the eyes of all men, secrets which may not be revealed, and which no man has discovered, but these secrets are lawful and honourable to know *by Masons*, who *only* have the keeping of them to the end of Time. (author's italics)

'Today we are here assembled in the presence of you all to build a House for Masonry which we pray God may prosper — if it seem good to Him, that it may become a Building for good men and good deeds, and promote harmony and Brotherly Love till the world itself shall end.'

These words uttered in the open air before a large crowd of persons, and of whom a great many neither were nor were ever able to become freemasons, must impress the modern listener with their clarity of intention and the dignity of their purpose. They are words that could well be expressed to not a few who in a later climate of public opinion have doubted the integrity or social usefulness of the masonic brotherhood. However, there was one more part of the ceremony on this occasion which might also give pause for reflection and some wonderment.

The architect having produced the plans for the PGM to inspect, the Deputy PGM addressed the Worshipful Master of Silurian Lodge:

'W Master, what will your lodge be like?' (He did of course mean *lodge room*.)

'The WM gave no answer, but pointed up to the heavens, then down to the earth and then extended his hands, pointing horizontally.

'DPGM: This is a good plan, but what have you more to tell me?

'The WM made no answer, but placed his right hand on his heart, and afterwards his left to his lips.

'The DPGM: the Master does well. Brethren let us copy his example.

'Each brother then gave the same signals.'

It only remained for the Provincial Grand Chaplain to offer prayer before the actual consecration took place and to say amongst much else —

'May (our) secret assemblies be convened in Law, proceed in Honour, and end in Charity. May all Masons that enter under the shadow of (this) roof remember that the secret of the Lord is with them that fear Him.

'O Lord! . . . teach us in all times and in all places to build up in beauty that Temple of our Soul which thou hast given us to adorn with all good works . . .'

When such sentiments and honourable longings attended the inauguration of this building it is not surprising to feel, even today, a real sense of peace and calm as one enters and shares its riches. It was surely no mere coincidence that following such a day there should be a move to found yet another lodge in Newport — Isca. Unhappily the building was not completed in time for the Isca Lodge consecration to take place there but it was able to join in the celebration on 26 October 1856 when at last the parts of the Masonic Hall that we have just visited were dedicated after another service, this time at St Woolos Church, now the Cathedral, at the top of the town.

As the brethren occupied their new and imposing premises for the first time they would have ample occasion to recall the past history of Newport Freemasonry of which this new move was but the climax. Samuel Combs could recall for them members of Royal Cambrian Lodge who had known an earlier Newport in which there was an even earlier lodge — weak and intermittent as it

was, of Antients' Grand Lodge warranting and yet still mentioned in the Calendar of 1800. That meant that these new occupants of Dock Street Hall could see themselves as the inheritors of a Craft that had been in the neighbourhood for almost a century already. There were even stronger links and recollections.

On the cessation of the Royal Cambrian Lodge in 1830 its jewels and furniture remained in the hands of the last person to be its Junior Warden, Edmund Jones. It was to his house that there came the Worshipful Master and Senior Warden of the Silurian Lodge in September 1841 to inspect 'the jewels and paraphernalia belonging to the old Lodge, and assess the value of the same. The list mentions the jewels of the Master, Past Master, S Warden, J Warden, Treasurer, Secretary, Inner Guard, S Deacon, J Deacon and Outer Guard; three chairs, columns, pedestal, gavel, chisel, and 2 foot guage, Bible, Square and compass, Rough and Perfect Ashlar, Tracing Board, Square, Level, Book of Constitutions and by-laws, Collars, Cocked hats (sic), aprons and gloves, tyler's sword, dagger, Glasses, Dupes, Banner and pole, Lantern and Seal. What happened at the interview we do not know . . .' (*op cit* Collins. pp16f.) We do know that present at the interview was also Thomas Hawkins who had been in the chair of Royal Cambrian in 1819-20. It is also clear that as no other mention of obtaining such a mass of essential equipment is recorded elsewhere it was all transferred to Silurian Lodge for its use especially as some of the former Newport masons were also part of the new body. It was in a sense coming back home. Even the Bible, which was one item that at first did not come to hand, reappeared after some years and is now part of Silurian's inventory. Two of the cocked hats, no longer being needed, can be found in those museum cases of which we have already spoken.

The place in which these lodge furnishings were to be used was the Westgate Hotel where they were charged five shillings a night unless refreshments were required in which case the room was granted to them free. By August 1846 however a new venue was considered and the following resolution appears in the minutes:

'That the building in High Street in this town, formerly called the Masonic Hall, be taken for the purpose of holding our Lodge, upon the terms proposed, viz £30 per annum'.

It is this extract from the minutes which begins to make sense of another interesting feature in the present day masonic hall. It is a large block of stone let into the wall at the foot of the winding stone staircase near the old entrance to the premises. It is headed with a crossed square and compass having a square over a letter G at its centre. The wording is:

'*This extension of the office of the* South Wales Argus *was erected in 1923-4 on the site of the Masonic Temple used by the Freemasons of Newport from 3 July, 1821 till 1841, and again from 14 August 1846 till October 1858.*'
Its exact location in High Street is then given.

The latter period of time mentioned here is self-explanatory for the date 1858 was when the brethren of Silurian and Isca Lodges moved into their present building. Why the Masons were described as using the hall for 20 years when either their lodge was decaying or erased (1821-41) is possibly because, as we have seen, there were still ex-Royal Cambrian members at large in the town and possibly their right to the hall and their occasional use of it for other purposes led to the idea that it was still being used by them for masonic purposes. At any rate the Silurian brethren had one more cause to thank their predecessors for keeping a possible meeting place alive and letting them use it until Dock Street was acquired.

There is still one more part of the story to tell. In September 1842 permission was sought from Grand Lodge to allow the lodge to process, fully clothed, with bible, banner, ashlars and the three Great Lights to the opening ceremony of the Newport Dock. Allowed to do so they were joined by brethren of the Sussex Lodge of Bristol, from Monmouth and Cardiff. They assembled at 6am (sic), opened in the First Degree, read the Dispensation and were then given precedence in the general procession! On their return they closed the lodge, agreed to meet at 4pm for dinner and finally went home at 7pm. For the rest of the century Silurian Lodge was by some referred to as 'the Docks Lodge' because of this event, and also because seafarers, pilots and an increasing number of docks officials and workers joined its ranks. This in itself begins to answer the question, why should the lodge eventually decide to find its continuing home in the dock area?

That there was a need for a new home began to be evident in 1852 when a complaint was made by the tyler, Bro Rogers, that the Choral Society, which had asked permission to use the masonic hall for their practices, not only left their own benches around after use so that the tyler could not get the room ready for its main use but that members of this Society had damaged more permanent parts of the lodge furniture. At the same time it was clear that so many men from the sea or the docks were asking for admission that if they attended in larger numbers there would be no room to accomodate them. In April 1853 there was made a proposal that they should consider building a new masonic hall. On the same evening it was decided to hire an organ as music was considered more and more essential for the best conduct of the ceremonies. No wonder that they insisted on so good an instrument in their first new temple.

An Emergency Lodge was held on 10 January 1855 to consider a lease on a site in Ruperra and Dock Street, to form a building committee and to commence the collecting of funds. There was no delay. The plans were submitted in February, £870 had been collected by March and by June the PGM had agreed to attend the Dedication ceremony for the stone-laying.

This, however, is still not the end of the story. For we have only visited one part of the present day building. In an historic and aesthetic sense we have visited the most important part of Newport Masonic Hall but turn to the left as you enter the old main door, or walk through the old museum room and the doors at the far end of it, and you will come to what looks like an entirely separate building and certainly a more modern one.

It was in the early years of this century that it was decided that improvements had to be made to the dining accommodation, as can be well imagined with the steady growth of lodges meeting here. Plans were submitted for what was to be the MARTYN KENNARD room at first floor level though there was then no idea of creating the rear staircase that we see in place today. The kitchens below were improved but in order to serve the new dining area the 'dumb waiter' now seen in the museum was installed. This new extension provided what is today an ample foyer where brethren can easily assemble, and the smaller foyer or ante-room up a few stairs beyond. The room provided was able to seat about 90 people which was a considerable advance on the previous facilities.

Such were the arrangements for the next fifty years. By 1960 it was clear that much greater premises still were necessary following the growth of Masonry

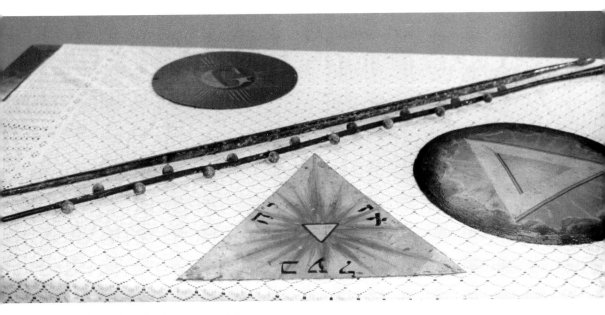

Rare examples of Aaron's Rod and some unusual plates.

locally after the war and thought had to be given as to whether the present site was the right one for such development. An attempt was in fact made to discover another location but in the event it was decided that an extensive alteration of the present building would be the best solution. Thus it was that the present large temple was added on the first floor using the earlier dining room for the preparation areas now seen. A new dining room was made below and the stairs that would give better access to the new upstairs areas at the rear were introduced. It is the result of these changes in 1960 that we now see and at least for the present we have the benefit of more modern amenities attached to an historic site.

The furniture in the large temple is naturally modern and functional with an arrangement, including pillars, that shows the continuity with that seen in the older parts of the building. For the largest meetings needed today and especially those associated with the Province it is ideal. It was no doubt a very commendable idea to move and doubless there were good reasons for considering it but it was propitious that the war ended such plans and the treasures of Dock Street were preserved for present masons to savour. It would have to be a fine architect indeed who could think of uprooting the present temples and restoring them elsewhere. In an age when at last we are properly respecting not only Victorian standards but their painting and architecture as well it is a privilege indeed to be able to visit Dock Street and all its hall contains.

PEMBROKE DOCK

(PORTHLADD BENFRO)

The Octagonal Temple

LOOKING DOWN FROM the northern ramparts of Pembroke Castle, the birthplace of a Tudor prince of England and Wales, the later Henry VII, one can still catch today a glimpse of the wholly rural surroundings of this late-12th century fortress when it was first constructed. Away to the left flows the Pembroke river on its way to form the Haven or safe anchorage for the largest of seagoing ships today, and on that river's northern shore, marked now with a crown of houses (Pennar) that stretch down to the Haven on its further side, there was, in the earliest days of the castle a quiet little farm settlement called Patrickchurch. We do not know exactly when it was first established but its name certainly suggests a mediaeval beginning and it may well have been named, if not started, at the time of the Norman occupation of these parts. What is certain is that until the year 1814 the village owned by the Adams family must have lived a simple and undisturbed existence under the protection of the great fortress just across the hill.

Down the Haven that flowed at its door the village dwellers would have seen growing activity at Milford where an attempt at creating a modern port was begun in and around 1800. But for another decade or so the village seems to have continued its undisturbed existence albeit there was also increased activity in the little repair yard at Neyland, or 'New Milford' as it was often called, directly across the water. Little could the ordinary dwellers of Paterchurch have guessed not only that they too were to be soon swallowed up in the effort to provide bigger and better men o' war, even though the final battle with Napoleon was not far off, but that even their village name was to disappear from the map of West Wales.

In 1814, when it was decided to close down Milford Haven as a naval dockyard the Admiralty selected this village with its sea front and promontory as the ideal alternative for their necessary work. Lord Nelson, who had long since urged the preference for Milford, was no longer alive to renew its claims on behalf of the Hamiltons, and as an up to date guide for the area makes clear the newly-named 'Pembroke Dock' was ideally suited for its more vigorous way of life.

'The deep sheltered water of the Haven and its location away from the European mainland made it an excellent "safe" base for experimentation with the new technology of shipbuilding — steam propulsion, iron cladding, screw and paddle propellers. For the rest of the century Pembroke Dock was probably the most advanced ship building yard in the world. In 1847 *Lion*, the largest warship in the Royal Navy, was launched. In 1852 the *Duke of Wellington*, the largest of the three-decked men o' war was completed. At the same time the nearby stone quay at Hobbs Point became the (new) packet point for the Cross-Channel Service to Ireland . . . In all, the dockyard built five Royal Yachts and a whole series of naval barques, brigantines, cruisers, gunboats and

Right: *Looking towards Senior Warden's Chair showing pillars and roof arch.*

The Master's pedestal and chair with plaster relief on the wall above.

battleships. By 1880 the yard was employing over 3,000 men and throughout World War 1 the dockyard worked to full capacity.' (Alan Shepherd: *A Visitor's Guide*. 1985. p78)

It is against this background of swiftly growing industry and population that we have to set the natural emergence of the Loyal Welsh Lodge, No 378 at Pembroke Dock. The presence of mariners and skilled craftsmen who would already be masons and who would wish to practice the Craft where they were now to be living and working soon revealed itself. Amongst the number of volunteers who came to the town in response to an invitation from the Admiralty in 1824, were three ardent freemasons from Devonport, William Hutchings, William Cook and John Chapple. They began meeting at the home set up by Mr Hutchings in Market Street but later met at the Porter Stores, at the top of Tregenna's Hill.

Later, in 1829, the lodge moved to the Navy Tavern which was even more appropriate for a lodge of this kind with its members' connection with honourable service of King (or Queen) and Country. The attractive badge of the Loyal Welsh Lodge, so well displayed inside the present masonic hall, shows a double towered entrance gate, with a symbolic 'Martello' tower above it and two red flags with Welsh dragons fluttering aloft. This was in fact the original badge of the Incorporated Borough of Pembroke, and the old dockyard here is still surrounded by its high walls of dressed limestone with the Victorian guntowers in place. You can even enter the port area, only now it is usually by car to join the B&I Ferry Terminal for Eire.

As the dockyard grew so did local Masonry. In 1833 the lodge moved to the Clarence Inn, thence to the Victoria Hotel in 1835, the house of a shoemaker in Meyrick Street and finally to the Royal Edinburgh Hotel. It was there that a completely separate lodge room was constructed for the brethren in 1857, a room which still exists with masonic emblems in relief on the hotel's outside walls. As the years passed however even this accommodation became inadequate and by 1869 they were moving to their first masonic hall in Bush Street. It is on that same site that they were to stay until the present time. Initially they constructed a two floored hall that looked in almost every respect as if it were a normal Nonconformist chapel, with a striking gabled west end, flanked by two pillared towers with upper lancet windows, and two other strong mullioned white stone windows to serve the temple and dining room. This in itself must have been a great advance for a lodge that was only 45 years old though it has to be recalled that a goodly number of those who were to enjoy its benefits were themselves craftsmen of a high order.

We know that by 1914 there were 134 subscribing members in the lodge and it is again therefore no surprise to learn that steps had already been taken to provide another even more ample 'home' for this large and vigorous craft unit. On a cold January afternoon in 1905 the new masonic hall was formally opened by H. G. Truscott and on the same day he installed his successor, Levi Phillips. The new building was designed by Messrs G. Morgan and Sons of Carmarthen and the contractor was a local man, Mr Charles Young, of Gwyther Street, Pembroke Dock. The estimated cost of the work was £1,500. Amongst those able to enjoy the procceedings was a Bro Matthew Nicholson of Dimond Street who had been the Worshipful Master as long ago as 1869.

As we today look at the outside of the hall in Bush Street we are seeing substantially the same building as was seen on that great occasion. There are even the same iron railings and gateway to protect the property and the same unashamed declaration that any passer-by can see. Over the gently curving stone arch that covers the recessed entrance porch there is a corbel-supported stone panel on which are inscribed the words 'M A S O N I C H A L L' and this is crowned with another semi-circle of stone bearing the square and compasses in their usual extended position. Only the extra pair of doors that now protects that inner porch have been added — a sad reflection on the greater need of security in our day.

The bush in the modest front garden is appropriate for it has grown from a cutting of an acacia plant, said to be grafted on to suitable rootstock and originally one of three trees. In a truly symbolic sense the present masonic hall has been raised from the ground in which this plant is found. On the corners of the two stone pillars already mentioned are two, now much worn down, foundation stones, one commemorating the start of the building and the other the opening and consecrating of the first masonic hall. The comparable stone for the large extension which we are to see is placed at the side of the arched porch that now adjoins the original building. On entering the latter we turn immediately left into what was the original hallway and can sense at once, with the solidity of the workmanship and the nature of the materials that we are back in the middle of the Victorian age. One can guess what it must have been like when the members were asembling for their meetings under the glow of a newly installed gaslight system.

Immediately opposite across this hall is a door that leads left into the one large assembly or committee room. It was originally used for dining and today is almost wholly devoid of any kind of ornament. Leaving this room we see opposite a steep flight of stairs which is completely boarded in with a downstairs toilet on one side and the cellar door with a committee room beside it on the other. The return flight to the landing and upper floor thus passes over the toilet. The access is compact but also gives the impression of being somewhat cramped. If previously the stairs from below simply led to the upper room, now used for dining, this is no longer the case. Turning off the narrow landing through a doorway we now find ourselves in a shallow, benched and oak fronted balcony looking down on to what is in fact an apparently octagonal inner temple. An entrance from the foot of the stairs below takes one into the same temple at the right hand end below the balcony.

It is this enormous room which was added in the later extensions of 1906, and it can at once be seen what a most impressive improvement it must have seemed to the brethren at that time. As it is we have yet another example of how the many craftsmen who belonged to this lodge determined that not only should their hall seem substantial from the outside but that it should be unusual within. Looking up immediately at the roof one is bound to be intrigued by the detail, colour and design that strike one as you see what is almost certainly an unique construction for such a hall. An eight-sided, vaulted dome of which there is but the slightest hint from the exterior view. The fact that this room lies so much to the rear of the earlier structure and is covered with interlocking tiles disguises what within would seem like a miniature dome over the crossing of a St Paul's Cathedral.

In this temple there is no pendant 'G' for the symbol of the Almighty is the great golden boss that lies at the central apex of the dome, surrounded by a halo of golden encrustation. This feature lies within an octagonal wooden frame that forms the source of the wooden ribs of the dome that drop in a curve to the inner ceiling level of the temple. Around the octagonal frame is a large expanse of gold paint with alternate rays and flames of gold forming the likeness of a 'glory' and drawing down one'e eyes to the blue firmament around it in which the stars in their usual astronomical arrangements are displayed. As might be expected it is the stars as may be seen from this hemisphere and such as the mariners in the lodge would be all too familiar with.

The actual stars in the sky are then surrounded, at the base of the dome, with a large foliate frieze in which are set, in alternate sequence, single and pairs of devices revealing the Zodiac and these again in their properly arranged order. Thus, in one single feature in the lodge, the visitor is reminded of his necessary faith in God, the work of the Great Architect and the ancient understanding of the knowledge of the universe with which our earliest forefathers were acquainted. It is a most remarkable piece of work for the lodge room of but one lodge.

Yet this is by no means all. Between the wooden base of the dome and the outer walls that support it through projecting beams there are flat ceiling areas of blue and white squares on which are depicted appropriate symbols for the persons who would normally sit beneath these areas. They are, of course, eight in number. Passing round them in a clockwise direction they are an open square for the WM, crossed wands for the Director of Ceremonies, a Bible within a glory for the Chaplain, a flying Dove for the deacons, a level for the Senior Warden, a plumb for the Junior Warden, crossed keys for the Treasurer and a Past Masters's square for those who have been Installed. All these symbols are drawn in full colour on a white or blue background and then set within a circle of red foliage with white edging.

The lessons to be learnt in this temple, however, have by no means finished with this decoration. We turn now to the eight walls beneath each of the separate octagonal sections of the dome. These are either planned as flat plain

Part of octagonal dome showing signs of the Zodiac along the rim; spandrels with cardinal virtues; Masonic symbols of Chaplain, Treasurer and Senior Warden, placed (as near as convenient) immediately above the Chairs occupied by those Officers. Similar devices are above the Chairs of the Worshipful Master, the Secretary and the Junior Warden.

wall surfaces, above the dark panelling of the back-to-wall seating, with a semicircular arch above a false stone-framed window, *or* as an indented wall surface with curved upper areas leading to yet another semicircular arch above. We thus realise that in fact the basic foundation of the room is square and it is by this ingenious change of wall pattern that the overall impression of an octagonal room is conveyed. What confirms the impression is the next range of decorative symbols that have been painted in colour on the spandrels between the curves of the arch and projecting beams that support the upper roof.

These corner emblems are very much in the style of the late pre-Raphaelite school of Victorian painting and are, in their way, a modern version of so much that some older 18th century lodges were able to display on their tracing cloths. The sequence, starting this time with those over the arch above the Senior Warden's chair are:

A snake   for Prudence
A sword and scales   for Justice

A mirror and lamp	for Truth
An alms bag	for Relief
A cross	for Faith
An anchor	for Hope
A radiant red heart	for Charity
A green leaf	for Temperance
A bunch of lilies	for Virtue
A Greek temple	for Honour
A sword	for Mercy
A key	for Secrecy
A hound	for Fidelity
A pair of stone tablets	for Obedience
A pair of open hands	for Brotherly Love

These, one can well imagine, are a very fruitful source of meditation for any whose minds may wish to wander a little in the course of our usual ceremonies. Certainly they are as valuable an aid to masonic teaching as any that can be conceived of elsewhere and the delicacy with which they are executed also adds to their worth. It might also be a matter for interesting reflection to see whether the designer's types for Temperance, Honour and Fidelity might have been replaced with even more apt parallels.

Allowing our gaze to drop still further we now remark that the semi-pillars from which the arches spring have at the cornice level decorations of acacia and corn plants. It is as we examine one or two of these decorations that mark the joints between the walls and the beams that support the ceiling that we can see the effect of damp and share something of the burden that the brethren bear in trying to maintain this exceptional building. Happily the Loyal Welsh Lodge is no longer alone in carrying the task of supporting the cost of this hall for in 1878 the Castlemartin Lodge was formed and in 1894 the Loyal Welsh Chapter. Even with the Penfro Mark Lodge sharing the expense after its formation in 1948 it has to be recognised that many of the brethren in the other orders are likely to belong to the local Craft membership and the circle of those who can carry the increasing expense of preserving so real a heritage as this hall must be limited.

We have not come to the end of the features that mark this hall, said to have been modelled on a Greek temple, as distinctive and memorable. Mention has already been made of the fact that the original seating, still in place, was of the 'backs to the wall' type so that as much space as possible was available for the ceremonies. More people have had to be accommodated since those days and there is now some additional seating in blue vinyl along the parquet flooring and around the huge tiled area of chequered paving that occupies most of the ground space. The officers' places however were constructed to fit in with the original design and there are no separate chairs for them. Whilst their places have arms and a well-constructed semicircular headpiece, each one bearing its own special golden emblem, the principal places are very much part of the whole lodge seating and thus the pedestals in front of them do not project unnecessarily into the floor area. They are however set on one, two and three steps respectively.

The pedestals and candlesticks whilst not being in any way exceptional are fine works of local craftsmanship. The candlesticks are mainly of the usual column form but they have one distinctive addition — they are set on small barrels or kegs — surely a touch that links them with a seafaring centre and perhaps indicates a naval carpenter at work. The pedestals are handsome pieces of mahogany with two strong pillars set in relief on both sides of the front panel. The panels have a rectangular groove also on the face and within this panel there is inlay of the Master and Wardens' tools. It is noteworthy that no extra columns with globes adorn these Wardens' desks.

On the other hand, as you stand before the Senior Warden's place your eyes are drawn to the two huge brown marbled pillars that flank his chair and stand against the corner pillars of the building. Topped with their celestial and terrestrial globes they reach up to the cornice moulding — some 12ft or more high.

Balancing these pillars alongside the Worshipful Master's chair are the banners of the Loyal Welsh and Castlemartin Lodges, the former in light blue and gold and the latter mainly dark blue and white. Over the Master's chair and affixed to the wall is the Loyal Welsh emblem that was referred to earlier but this is also flanked by two unusual lists of Loyal Welsh Masters which merit more detailed study. Of late Victorian design and only some two feet in height they comprise a list of all the Past Masters of the lodge but with the names since 1905 actually added in their own handwriting. These simple frames, with two carved columns on three steps at the sides, and with a carved metal strip above them in the form of a shallow arch, were presented to the lodge after the opening of the new hall in 1906. On the back of the frame with the earlier names there is the following statement:

'LOYAL WELSH LODGE 378 of Freemasons

Bas-Relief above Master's Chair of Loyal Welsh Lodge No 378.

This frame was presented to the above Lodge by Bro B. Mules, J.W. 1871. It is made from the following historically connected woods: the bases are from an old lintel brought from one of the old temples in Palestine; the Pillars and arch are part of an old beam from the Cathedral of St David's; the small frame on top of the arch is from a portion of HMS *Bellerophon*, which conveyed Napoleon I to England, and contains the likeness of the first Master of the Lodge, the late PM Dr Thomas.

'The two metallic strips are part of the Atlantic cable which conveyed that truly Masonic message from Her Majesty the Queen Victoria to President Abraham Lincoln of America "Glory to God on High, Peace on Earth and Goodwill towards men".'   Designed by Bro P. M. Neil Boyle. PPGP

Of such apparently ordinary and easily overlooked items in a hall is true history made. The idea of continuing to ask men to sign their names for posterity and in frames which carry so many thoughtful links with the past is in itself most worthy of commendation. Whilst some might easily dismiss these items as mere Victorian bric-a-brac they have in their place here as modern a relevance as all the other features that surround them.

One of the Past Masters honours boards for Loyal Welsh Lodge No 378. All Masters since 1824 have signed the roll.

Around the temple room just below the domed ceiling are symbols and painted windows. Shown here are Faith, Hope and Charity.

No less impressive are the large post-Union but original 1824 tracing boards that are now curtained or displayed according to the degrees which are conducted in this room. As has been said elsewhere in this volume the features of all tracing boards merit careful study for those who assume that all boards are identical have either never given them careful thought or close scrutiny. The boards here, especially those in the 2° and 1°, repay such attention. It is alleged that they may have been stolen from St David's Lodge No 366 when that lodge was in decline.

Looking up from the floor of the lodge above the organ that fits so neatly into the walled seating, and the Secretary's marked chair that is alongside it, one now sees the pleasant pillared balcony to which we first took our way. This provides ample space for the biggest installation or consecration ceremonies and yet brings an element of warmth and diversity into what is already an intriguing temple. To look down from this place upon any ceremony that takes its course below must be an unusual experience. But, then, a visit to the hall at Pembroke Dock is itself something not to be forgotten. It is much to be hoped that this hall will be able to continue to fascinate visitors into Loyal Welsh and Castlemartin's second centuries.

Such a wish is all the more heartfelt when it is learnt that the hall might not have survived the last Great War. During that conflict many convoys were assembled in the safety of the Haven and the town had a major additional role as a fuel and supply base. These activities, together with its usefulness as a centre for co-ordinating coast protection work, attracted heavy enemy bombing attacks and the people here courageously endured far more damage and civilian casualties than any other town in the area. The masonic hall did not go unscathed. Visible to this day on the outside roof and just visible as a scar on the blue ceiling of the dome, almost above where the Master has his place, is the result of a large piece of shrapnel that fell on the building but only caused superficial damage. Incendiaries or a direct hit could so easily have been the alternative to this less dangerous damage and then the future of the hall would certainly have been in doubt. As it is we have it still and long may it continue to serve the orders of Masonry for the future.

SWANSEA

(ABERTAWE)

The Hall with the 'Indefatigable' Story

THE MASONIC HALL in St Helen's Road is another storehouse of local treasures. Carefully preserved within its walls are many heirlooms of its past – banners, portraits, symbols and old documents. Of the latter one of the most precious is the warrant that was presented to the masons of Swansea in 1844 by Mr John Gwyn Jeffreys, a local solicitor. It had been lost sight of for almost 40 years following the decline of the Beaufort Lodge (originally numbered 443) in 1805 and it was only due to the action of this non-mason that we have here an invaluable token of Swansea's earliest masonic activity. The warrant itself has two particularly interesting features. The first is that it bears the name and titles of the 'Moderns' Grand Master in 1769 after whom it was decided to name the lodge – 'WE Henry Somerset Duke of Beaufort, Marques (sic) and Earl of Worcester, Earl of Glamorgan, Viscount Grosmont, Baron Herbert Lord of Raglan, Chepstow and Gower, and Baron Beaufort of Caldicot Castle, Grand Master....'. As this noble lord was a member of the family which had been for a long time the hereditary Lords of Swansea and Gower and was then 'paramount in directing the destinies, and in appointing the principal officers of the corporation, of our borough' the lodge's title was almost certainly chosen as a compliment to him. The warrant, however, bears the number 378 and this would seem to be at variance with the number already given and recorded in the 'Engraved List' for 1769. However, we discover that some delay in paying the necessary fees to Grand Lodge for the issue of the charter meant that it was not in fact transmitted until after February 1770 by which time one of the occasional alterations in numbering English warranted lodges had again occurred. The newly allocated number was therefore that which now adorns the warrant which Swansea masons possess. The altered number shows, moreover, that whilst a warrant was then essential for the ongoing work of the lodge it was not necessary for the lodge's inauguration, as it would be today.

As William Henry Jones has recorded in his first history of the advancement of Freemasonry in Swansea the founders of this first local lodge 'were, necessarily already Freemasons, and probably were either new-comers and comparative strangers to the town, or master-mariners or travellers whose avocations brought them at regular intervals to Swansea.' Nonetheless a local Secretary had been appointed before the first year was up, Gabriel Jeffreys, and they could hardly have been better served than by this first clerk to the harbour trustees, pioneer of the Swansea canal, Portreeve (or Mayor) and promoter of the Mumbles railway in 1804. He at least knew how to get on with the Grand Lodge in London for a letter from that quarter in 1770 acknowledges receipt of '3 Barrels of Oysters which were very good, and for which I am much obliged to you'.

Right: *Entrance to the Masonic Hall at Swansea. It was originally two villas in the gardens of which were built the Connaught Hall and Refectory with temples above.*

The Major Temple opened in 1926. The Master's chair was the gift of Caradoc Lodge No 1573 at their 50th jubilee in 1926.

Interestingly the Secretary lived in Wind Street where stood the Star Tavern, home of the only post-chaise in this part of Wales and also the place where the lodge first met. Since the lodge rose to 20 members in a very short time it was decided to move to the more spacious Mackworth Hotel. Here the lodge began to fit itself out with a whole range of furniture including three mahogany armed chairs with 3, 2 and 1 step respectively for the Master and Wardens, 4 mahogany columns, pomegranates of gilt, 28 wands painted pure white (which were probably used when the brethren paraded to church), candlesticks and much else. It was the start of a grand idea!

In June 1770 Bro Jeffreys tells the Grand Secretary that he is contemplating 'a suitable home for Masons in Swansea' and thus applies for 'the plan of the Grand Lodge at London, and likewise a plan for a lodge (here) which I have begun but must have your assistance to go through with'. Sadly the plan was not persisted with and in 1801 the lodge returned to the more constricting premises of the Lamb Inn in Wind Street. By 1805 it was in decline and in 1809 it had been wound up and its right to a warrant transferred to a new lodge named St John's No 327 which is still working in Wigton, Cumbria.

Gabriel Jeffreys, however, as Past Master and the then present Senior Warden of the Beaufort Lodge had already played his part in securing a much more stable future and enduring life for Freemasonry in his native town. This he did by acting as Consecrating Officer for a new lodge in Neath, with two brethren from the Beaufort Lodge actually becoming founders of the new body. Since these Beaufort brethren already met in the Mackworth Arms it may have appealed to them to be associated with this new 'Gnoll Lodge' which was named after Gnoll House, the home of the local Lord of the manor, Sir Herbert Mackworth. (The name is very familiar to the author since he used to visit people as a curate on the Mackworth estate on the outskirts of Derby from which this family originally came.) Sir Herbert himself was to become an initiate in Gnoll Lodge in 1779.

Though the lodge at Neath was supported in its first decade by very substantial local figures as members it appears by 1787 to have begun a steady change in its fortunes and by 1800 Swansea men who were eager to have membership of a Moderns lodge so as to form a new one in their own town were joining at Neath. Indeed in this same year the lodge had been transferred to the 'Plume of Feathers' Inn in Swansea and its future was to lie in this new and growing port. Of Neath and Masonry we have heard elsewhere. By 1804, when the first extant minute book begins with the St John's Festival in December, the Gnoll Lodge had disappeared and the name had changed to the present one of 'Indefatigable'. Following the demise of the earlier Beaufort Lodge after 1805 the name was actually given as 'The United Indefatigable and Beaufort Lodge' but 'this was never regularised at Grand Lodge and after several changes of mind it was finally decided in 1848 that the style should in future be "Indefatigable Lodge" alone.' (*Bicentenary brochure.*)

It is this lodge to which so much in the present masonic hall pays tribute, and it was largely due to the members of this lodge in particular that the continuance of Freemasonry in Swansea was for long maintained. Eventually they combined with the five other lodges that grew up in the town – Talbot 1323 (1870), Caradoc 1573 (1874), Dr James Griffith Hall 3161 (1906), Beaufort 3834 (1918) and Penrice 4172 (1920) – to procure and build the present premises. Their progress to the happy situation in which Swansea masons currently find themselves did, however, require in a literal sense that they should be indefatigable masons. A brief survey of their meeting places alone explains why.

Eager to have a more ample meeting place for their growing membership and the use of some of the equipment brought after the ending of the Beaufort the members moved from the Tiger Inn on the Strand to the Mackworth Arms. They had to do legal battle to regain their furniture from the Tiger's landlord (though he was also a brother) and even when they had settled at the the Beaufort meeting place they soon found out, as had probably begun to be clear earlier to their predecessors, that the advent of better coaching services and the new Mumbles railway was making the 'Mackworth' too busy for the masons to meet as they wished. They again thought about a room of their own. This was even more encouraged as an idea when, during a Provincial Grand Lodge 'meeting' at the hotel the 'family of the landlord passed through the room to bed'. Whilst trying other inns and taverns without success and even gathering in the newly provided Assembly Rooms in Cambrian Terrace, no lasting solution

The Minor Temple with the two pillars that came from Bristol in 1837 for three pounds.

was reached, especially when in 1849 the original tesselated floor-cloth, that probably also served as the tracing board, was seized and disposed of for recovery of debt incurred by the lessor. A sideboard that was also purchased to enable the brethren to have a more satisfactory storage place for books, smaller items of crockery and also the means of refreshement, was kept and is now in the lounge of the present hall.

Besides this latter item a visitor to the hall today can conjure up many pictures of the lodge and its meetings in these first 60 years of the oldest Swansea lodge's existence. Here, for instance, will be found the warrant of confirmation issued in May 1805, by Frances Rawdon, Earl of Moira, Acting Grand Master. There is the large and well preserved early banner presented by Sir Christopher Cole, KCB, in 1821 and then kept in use until 1881. Sir Christopher had the unique experience of being initiated, passed and raised on the one night, 23 October 1817 and from 1821 was nominated by the lodge to fill the position of Provincial Grand Master for what was then the combined Province of South Wales.

This banner is seen as one mounts the main staircase and on the walls of the half-landing there hangs an equally imposing portrait of a roundfaced, kindly figure, seated in a leather armchair, with black suit, white kerchief and thin-rimmed spectacles. This was Dr George Gwynne Bird who was initiated, passed and raised in 1829. He was a distinguished member of the medical profession, wrote a standard work on cholera after his service in the Swansea Infirmary and was not a little responsible for finding a cure for this malady by instituting new methods of hygiene.

Besides being Master of the lodge in 1832 and 1845 he was also Deputy Provincial Grand Master from 1851 to 1863, Mayor of Swansea in 1842 and 1843 and a Justice of the Peace in 1844 when he took an active part in suppressing the Rebecca rioters who objected to the imposition of toll charges on the turnpikes. A local artist was commissioned by the people of Swansea to paint his portrait since he was so well regarded and it was the members of his Indefatigable Lodge who completed the charges for it. In 1856 WBro Bird asked that the portrait should hang in the lodge room where he had spent so many hours in peace, harmony and retirement.

Turning along the wide landing that leads from the top of the main stairs one's attention is held by the well filled display cabinets that line most of the walls on the right. At the foot of a case well filled with jewels there is suspended a broadsword with a most distinctive cockle shell decorating it below the hilt and at the top of the blade. This was presented to the lodge by Bro Matthias of Pembrokeshire in 1805 and was then stated to have been taken from the hand of a Frenchman in the act of chopping down a native of Fishguard. This of course was part of that abortive invasion by French troops in 1797. Alongside this weapon there are some priceless and unique Royal Arch jewels which are said to date from 1771. They belong to the Virtue and Hope Chapter formed in Swansea after much negotiation in March 1812 and it would seem that the 'indefatigable' Gabriel Jeffreys must have purchased these at that time since he wrote in 1770 to the Grand Secretary asking if such a Chapter could be established. It was not to happen in 'Beaufort's time' but at least the later brethren had jewels to wear as Principals even if, as we learn, they had to wait two years or more for their robes.

In a display case on the wide landing we shall find a sample of the lodge china punch bowls with masonic emblems decorating it in blue. Beside the name of the RW Master (sic) of the time – W. Essery – there is a Swan on water representing the town and below it the date on a scroll, AL5806. Around the bowl on the outside appear the Blazing Sun, the Moon and seven stars, the 3 Great Lights and the working tools of the three degrees. Beside it stands an ewer of white china with what look like transfers in blue of exactly the same style and date of those on the bowl. The firing glasses close by are of a fairly common pattern with their short holders and stubby bases but have their own distinction in being variously numbered 237, 288 and 427 as the Indefatigable Lodge was re-numbered during the years.

In this same display case which was given to the hall by Dr James Griffith Hall Lodge there are further mementoes of this early Regency and Victorian age in the form of a charming glass jug etched with the open book, two pillars, a trowel, mallet and crossed square and compasses, but above all the name of Bro R. Trevithick, the contemporary railway locomotive builder, who may have been involved in the local railway developments and visited this lodge. A charming elegant cut glass goblet with beehive emblems and a pentagram with G at its centre is another clue to what adorned their festive board.

Turning off this corridor into one of the Committee rooms, with its elegant and solid furniture, one comes across another three items of the early period. One of these is a silk banner displaying the arms of the 'new' United Grand Lodge embraced by what look like two huge sprigs of acacia and leek and having across their head the scroll with the words in Latin, 'Spectemur Agendo' (May we be noted for our deeds). This is one of a pair that were painted and presented to the lodge in 1818 by Bro John Francis who was a coachbuilder and clever heraldic painter. He never took the chair of Indefatigable Lodge though he joined it in 1815, but he later became Provincial Grand Secretary. In the letter he wrote for the presentation he added the delightful words, 'I trust that they will ever be a powerful excitement (sic) to unite you on a Foundation that may not be shaken by any of the trivial occurrances of the too oft discords we all are liable to fall into.'

In the Smaller Temple there is a noteworthy coffin lid, painted in 1821 and almost certainly by Bro Francis, which teaches its own lesson with the emblems of mortality at its head, a large winged hour-glass at the centre over the word in capitals 'REMEMBER' (referring to a certain Bible passage) and below an open Bible. If the brethren did at one point have trouble with finding a

The Major Temple, Swansea.

satisfactory lodge floor cloth they certainly never ceased to have the right emblems for the third degree.

Rich and varied then as are the links between the present day and those of the first days of the Indefatigable Lodge in Neath and Swansea – with the same Volume of the Sacred Law printed in 1754 and only once rebound, the same silver square and compasses of 1812 upon it, and a snuff box and spirit measure occasionally brought out for use – the brethren of the late 1850s were even more determined to find a home of their own. They started a register for donations and shares and they looked at many sites, with an old synagogue, a corporation plot and a too expensive private building space all being considered. By 1871 however they had chosen an area of land in Caer Street and on 6 July the ceremony of laying the foundation stone duly took place. Provincial Grand Lodge was held in the Mackworth Arms Hotel at noon, the brethren processed in full regalia through the streets to the site and with clergy and ladies in attendance the stone was laid with all due ritual and ceremony. The proceedings were brought to a close, we are told, at an early hour. The hall built on the site was to be used until 1926 when the present hall was formally opened.

We are provided with ample evidence of what the hall at Caer Street looked like and it is worth noting that though the construction was carried out by William Thomas, William Watkins and David Jenkins, who were known as 'The Firm', none of these men were masons until three years later when they were all initiated on the same evening. The room they created for the temple was most impressive with a lofty, ecclesiastical timbered ceiling, ample space for movement on the ground, sufficient space in the east for a large canopied chair and pedestal and two huge fluted columns with framed globes atop them, and a magnificent organ gallery with its globe-capped oaken casing for the console under a huge pillared arch from under which the rays of the sun at its setting filtered down.

It is again possible to imagine some of the atmosphere of this very Victorian room by looking at the well-padded leather officers' chairs that are now kept in one of the side rooms at St Helen's Road. Here is quality with permanence and is is hardly surprising that for several years this furniture continued to be used in the smaller temple of the latest premises until something more suitable was decided upon for the present age. The fluted pillars with their globes have been reproduced in the smaller temple here at the north-east and south-east corners of the room whilst on the walls of this temple one can also see the heavy brass symbols that once marked the desks of the Secretary and Treasurer in Caer Street. Also in use is the hinged and folded mahogany tracing board which is placed flat on the tesselated flooring in the centre of the small temple. This painted 'set of boards' is unique and very old. It is, of course, removed when other than Craft degrees are worked.

The need for larger premises still was recognised as early as 1907 when property adjoining the Caer Street Hall was purchased and thought was given to the possibility of enlarging and redesigning the lodge room. By now the population of Swansea had increased greatly and the work offered in the new dock installations and Copper Works nearby meant that there was ample scope for new lodges. The Talbot Lodge had appeared in mid 1870, the Caradoc Lodge in 1874, and the Dr James Griffith Hall Lodge in 1905/6. Yet whilst there was a need for growth in the size of the hall it proved to be an impossible venture and with the advent of the First World War the idea was shelved. The consecrations of the Beaufort Lodge (new version) in 1917 and the Penrice Lodge in 1920 were to start again the plans for a separate development especially as these new units requested Indefatigable Lodge for space to meet. With real foresight a few Past Masters and officers of the lodge purchased in 1922 the house and grounds known as Brunswick House and all the existing local lodges were invited to join in the venture that produced the present new hall in St Helen's Road.

The new Swansea Masonic Hall Company was formed in April 1923 with mortgage debentures to raise money and in May the Trustees of Indefatigable Lodge were instructed to convey to the new Company the proceeds of the sale of the Caer Street buildings and site. Those buildings in fact continued until they were destroyed by enemy bombing on 1 September 1940, and were not in fact disposed of legally until after the war was over. In September 1926, however, a service of dedication for the new hall was held at St Mary's Parish Church when the preacher was the Rev Canon Cecil Wilson, Vicar of Swansea and Junior Warden of the Penrice Lodge. The service was followed by the ceremony at the new hall, conducted by the Provincial Grand Master and his officers. The new Master's chair was given by Caradoc Lodge, 1573, which was commemorating its jubilee.

It is difficult today to imagine in a busy town street that where this large masonic hall stands was once the site of two villas with their gardens. Having made a present to the Corporation of part of their original frontage so that the road could, when required, be widened the masons have now found themselves with inadequate parking space in a very different world. Nonetheless the absence of too many cars does permit the visitor to appreciate the fine flight of ten steps that leads to an open stone area before the house façade and its fine porticoed entrance door. The plain Ionic columns flank three shallow steps and the neo-Gothic oak doorway which has above it a rising sun with its rays topped by an interrupted triangular pediment. This is further enhanced by the stained glass windows above in rectangular casements, the designs of which can best be seen from the landing within. The whole exterior in well set but rough cast stone work, with gentle stone arches over each window or entrance, gives a sense of solidity and quality. It is a worthy haunt for craftsmen.

Rooms in the front of the building which are linked by a very wide staircase comprise crush hall, cloak rooms, committee and rehearsal rooms whilst over what were the rear gardens have been erected the dining halls with a main and a

Below left: Glass Goblet with masonic symbols, one of many items in the Display Case at Swansea Masonic Hall.

Below: Some of the stained glass windows in the Crush Hall leading to the Temples and Committee rooms of the Swansea Masonic Hall.

Below right: Glass Jug, etched 'BRO R TREVITHICK', together with Seven Stars and Crescent Moon and the Square and Compasses with two Pillars and other symbols at the sides. Richard Trevithick was born in Cornwall in 1771. In 1801 he built a locomotive which carried passengers along a road. He later built high-pressure steam engines used for many purposes. In 1816 he was in Peru building mining engines. He died in poverty in 1833 and a memorial service was later held in Westminster Abbey.

Royal Arch Jewels, probable date 1771, belonging to Virtue and Hope Chapter No 237, Swansea. The Grand Secretary in 1927 stated that they were valuable and that none like them were held in Grand Lodge.

minor temple above. At the top of the two flights of stairs stands the window already seen from below. It is a restrained but still colourful display, with three roundels in the upper casements, two having pentalphas and one showing an open bible with the compasses on a set square. Below these are the three arms of lodges that occupied these premises after their opening – Corinthian Lodge, 4917 (1927), Glantawe Lodge, 5378 (1932) and Penllegaer Lodge, 5567 (1935). Their designs give an immediate sense of quality and involvement to what is already a place of history and local association.

Turning to the left along the corridor already mentioned we find ourselves soon at seven wide steps leading up to a spacious landing and foyer outside the main temple. 'Silence' is the order plainly indicated and the sumptuous Past Masters' boards, the well upholstered leather benches along one wall (another relic of Caer Street) and the further row of stained glass 'tools' which act as a 'dormer' to this anteroom area all contribute to keeping that request.

Thence we pass into the main temple which is tastefully and grandly designed with pure white surfaces, clusters of paired Corinthian columns around the walls and a fine inlaid tesselated area stretching almost the full length of the room. Upon it and at its centre stands the elegant tracing board case on fine carved and claw grip legs and around it are commodious and comfortable looking armchairs of wood and leather. Most striking of all are the huge pendant gold 'G' at the centre of the room, the huge bejewelled 'eye' above with a circle and rays flanked by two large compasses and squares in the FC position, and the arrangement at the Master's place.

This comprises a large light oak chair which is designed to resemble the portico through which we first entered the building. It must be at least 12ft high. Towering over it is a contraption of wood with a rope hanging within a frame, for all the world at first sight like a partly concealed guillotine. It is in fact a device for raising a banner of whichever lodge is at labour. Behind this contraption and applied in gilt upon the upper rear east wall is a glorious representation of the rising sun which contrasts effectively with the pure white wall and columns around it. Yet most striking of all and closely flanking the large Master's chair are two equally high and rounded Egyptian pillars with lotus decoration, pomegranates and the two usual globes at their head.

The main places of the Master and his Wardens in this temple are further marked by two other well designed features. These are the steps leading up to each dais on which an officer sits, five for the Master, three for the Senior and three for the Junior Warden – an interesting variation on the more usual 3, 2 and 1. Furthermore, at each place, there stands a most elegant candlestick in one of the usual architectural styles with with 7 chequered grades to the base of the one at the Master's right, 5 to the one of the Senior Warden and 3 at that of the Junior, in all a most salutary reminder to the lodge of the natural progression through which each mason may pass. It is hardly surprising that the overall impression is one of great symmetry and thoughtful significance.

This impression is confirmed when we pass from the main to the minor temple in this building. The decor here is simpler, without any columns along the walls, but this gives even greater prominence to the two great pillars with their framed globes which have been mentioned already. What was not then said is that these pillars were purchased from Bristol in 1837 for the sum of £3. Their value today is infinitely greater for they represent over 150 years of continuous existence and symbolism in this latest home of Swansea Masonry. In this room as also in the other the ceiling carries the 'All-Seeing Eye', the square and compasses and a large crescent moon with its seven stars. This latter reference to the Great Architect is also reinforced by the similar portrayals of the rising and setting sun that adorn the walls over the Master and Senior Warden's places.

What is yet one more connection with the past is the set of pedestals still used here. The Master's is thought to have been provided in 1813 and then to have been fitted with three locks, like old churchwardens' trunks, so that it could not be opened and its contents displayed or used until three came together to agree to unlock it. In this case too the Wardens also had a key.

Before we bid farewell to this veritable storehouse of old masonic memories and traditions we ought to pause at the door of the lounge and examine the round escutcheon that is placed there. It is a relic of a 'Grand Orient of France Lodge' which, though unrecognised by London, worked in Swansea under the name of the Tawe Lodge until that name being taken by the local Workhouse the lodge changed its title to 'Harmony'. Regular masons were warned against supporting it in 1894 and 1902 but it was able to survive until 1926 when, on the new hall being available, some of its members joined one of the regular lodges at

This Sword was presented to the Indefatigable Lodge No 237 (then numbered 333) in 1805 by Brother Mathias of Pembrokeshire who stated that it had been 'taken from the hand of a Frenchman in the act of chopping down a native of Fishguard' in the abortive French invasion in 1797.

The ceiling of the Minor Temple at Swansea.

St Helen's Road. Here then is yet one more surprising link with masonry's local past. What is not surprising is the affection in which these long desired premises are held by those who come to practise their Masonry here. They look with pride upon their past and with no less vigour continue to build up a tradition for the future.

However, ample as the premises were when opened with 6 lodges in 1926 the present occupation of this building by 23 lodges, 12 Royal Arch Chapters and 10 associated degrees, apart from the lodges of Instruction, the committees and Ladies' Evenings, means that accommodation is once more a problem. Car parking in a central city area is also a difficulty not envisaged in 1926. Yet if this leads to new consideration of larger premises it is realised that it would be impossible in this day and age to reproduce at an acceptable cost the fine temples or even the historic ambience so evident in Swansea's present much loved home.

OTHER MASONIC HALLS IN SOUTH WALES

Neyland-Narberth-Tenby-Chepstow

NEYLAND

IT MAY NOT BE realised by many that Neyland could well have developed into the most notable embarkation point for travellers on what was the dream of 'God's Wonderful Railway' — GWR. From here they might make their way to Ireland, across to Shannon and thence on the biggest leg of the western trip — a ship passage that would bring the prairies of the USA within reach. 'Created as "Little Milford" in Napoleonic times, Neyland owes its origin to Sir Isambard Brunel, the famous railway engineer, who selected this site as a terminal of the projected South Wales to Manchester Railway. Following its establishment as a rail centre, Neyland became the terminal for the Irish Packet Service, and continued as such until 1906 when the Irish traffic was transferred to Fishguard.' (Official Guide.)

Once an important deep-sea fishing port the association with the Atlantic route is commemorated with a 'Great Eastern Terrace' which was so named because the SS 'Great Eastern' lay for a time here. There is an echo of the potential importance of Neyland in the 19th century when the Provincial Grand Lodge was held there in July 1881. Its meeting place was the waiting room of the local railway station, which must have been of more than the usual dimension.

By the same token the new importance of Pembroke Dock was being recognised and there are even notes in the lodge minutes of a proposal that the lodge be removed to that place. The lodge went on meeting in the ante-room of the South Wales Hotel until 1891, over a quarter of a century after its inauguration, when it was agreed to negotiate with Picton Castle about a site with a 35ft frontage at 1/- per foot. The minutes of 10 November that year are in part worth repeating: 'It was also decided to fix a stove on the left hand side of the lodge opposite the JW chair, that a raised platform be prepared for the Brethren and a raised dais for the Past Masters — wood seats or benches for the brethren and half circular for the Past Masters.' That arrangement is still there for all to see.

On 8 December a letter was received from Sir Charles Phillips of the Castle stating that he appreciated the good work of Freemasonry generally and that he would agree to the ground rent suggested and a term of lease for 99 years. That would bring it up to 1990. In February 1892 a lodge balance of £50 5s 0d was allocated for new lodge furnishings and it is here worth noting that up to this time most of the main lodge requirements had been met by moving items from the Cambrian Lodge at Haverfordwest every time there was a meeting.

Lord Kensington, the Provincial Grand Master of South Wales (Western Division) was present on 23 November 1892 when the hall was dedicated and said that he was very satisfied at 'being with them on the occasion of Neyland Lodge obtaining a home of their own and congratulated the members on the acquisition of a very beautiful lodge room.' (Centenary brochure by W. M. Childs) Two acacia trees were originally planted in the strip of land in front of the hall (cf Pembroke Dock) and as a memento of that opening of their premises there is still a special jewel, kept in a glass case, that was presented by the Neyland brethren to WBro S. J. Allen and inscribed thus: 'Presented . . . in token of their esteem and recognition of four years honourable and faithful service as Secretary during which the new Masonic Hall was so successfully inaugurated, built and dedicated, Neyland, December 1893.'

The hall is a modest affair that fits well with the locality. It makes no apology for its purpose and its outer facade is one of its fine features. It is made of local materials and has two fine corner pilasters with light blue decorated chapiters supporting a strong triangular pediment with light blue finials over its peak and the attendant pilasters whilst below it, picked out in white, are the square and compasses flanked by two pentacles. Below them an arched frieze surrounds another lesser triangular pediment over three front, blue-framed windows that gave light to the single ante-room and temple. One enters by a door to the right of this array.

In the ante-room is a bookcase containing the well-kept minutes of the lodge and from these we might read two extracts that give a flavour of the years that have passed. The first is from the neatly written if flowery language of Bro Neale in 1894. Writing about a brother who had just lost his wife he says:

'Bro X feelingly referred to the loss sustained by the removal from this temporary abode by Death's Dark Angel of a lady well known for her Christian Charity, profusely exercised.' In 1902 we have a letter received from the Grand Secretary referring to a practice that was also current in the lodge at Ludlow (see *Masonic Halls of England*, Midlands). The letter reads:

'It having been brought to the attention of the Board that on more than one occasion, at the Installation of the Master, wine has been introduced for the purpose of drinking his health I am directed by the Board to point out, what cannot be too widely known, that such practice is contrary to that feeling of Masonic propriety which holds the Lodge to be a sacred place and to remind the brethren that the appropriate occasion for showing such courtesy is at the subsequent Installation Banquet'

It is from the minutes of as early as 1898 that we learn of 'many attempts made to secure a canopy for use over the Master's chair but on each occasion caution prevailed and the matter was postponed sine die and has remained so to this day'. (Brochure) When we move into the temple we can see why they should have wanted to effect that addition so as to complete the impression of simple dignity for so charming a meeting place. Moreover one can see that the decorations done for the Centenary almost 30 years ago have been maintained with love and attention. The shallow bowed roof with its fine dark oak timbers has been painted in white largely,with a dark blue ceiling over the east end. A delightful decorated star of silver colour in the dark blue area is reflected by the lights down the centre of the room and they also show up the large gilt 'G' that hangs from the roof.

In the east the Master's very fine Victorian chair, of a slightly larger but similar design to those of the Wardens stands against a pure white wall niche that is capped by an arched rib with corbels at its two ends. With the polished red-cushioned straight and curved benches, the upright, wicker-back IPM's chair, the original tracing boards curtained or displayed in the east and the two large black and gilt Masters boards in the white niche, the effect is very moving in this small meeting place. When you further notice the red and blue chequered flooring of the dais, the black and white chequer on the plain dark blue carpet of the rest of the floor and then the light blue pilasters, with dark blue chapiters and white edgings, that support the beams, you realise that here is a hall that is much valued by its occupants.

Two other slight features that give this hall an added character are the presence of TWO Bibles on the pedestal and ledge in front of the Master. Moreover there is provision for three persons to kneel round this ledge at the same time. The other item is to remark that at each of the three main officers' places are the three tools that are associated with a different degree. The tools, in other words, are not in a special box by the Master's place but placed for use by the Master or his wardens in turn.

The terminal buildings, the large station and the even larger hotel built at Neyland specifically for Transatlantic passengers no longer exist and where they stood has now been developed into a very sophisticated yacht marina. The Western Division of South Wales, however, can take pride in a hall that has survived other changes of local fortune and which its masons both planned and have maintained with honour.

The very canopy that the masons of Neyland never achieved can undoubtedly be said to be the main feature and delight of the hall at Narberth. A description of it we shall come to in a few moments but it most certainly graces the lofty room that the masons here have converted into their temple after its earlier life as part of a Wesleyan chapel. Even before we describe it further or come to the story of how that occurred it might be as well to identify the town to which this lodge and hall belong.

NARBERTH/Yn Arberth

Narberth is in fact extremely old as a settlement and can trace its origins back to the Bronze Age. There is mention of it in the great Welsh classic work of the 'Mabinogion' where it is referred to as the place where Prince Pwyll of Dyfed had his principal palace. The first castle here was in 994 and after several rebuildings there was a castle which Cromwell failed to destroy during the Civil War and which was inhabited as late as 1657. Originally it was called Castell yn Arberth and it was only when South Pembrokeshire was anglicized that the town became known as Narberth.

The first lodge in the town was formed in 1883 by four men living locally, one of whom was from the Neyland Lodge, and the project was supported by the Cambrian Lodge No 464. It is not unimportant to record that the first Master of the lodge after its consecration at the De Rutzen Hotel, its first home, was the squire of Lamphey Court, Charles Mathias, Esq, whilst the first two wardens were a bank manager and a merchant. It is a sign of stability that the Master in the lodge's Centenary year was the great-nephew of the first Junior Warden. The lodge also got off to a busy start with fourteen candidates in the first year of whom all were passed and thirteen were even raised. To carry out these ceremonies the lodge had to borrow furniture from Cambrian Lodge as had the Neyland brethren but by 1884 some furniture and regalia of their own was able to be purchased so that the cost and trouble of the first borrowings were discontinued. In that same year the first banner of the lodge, still on the right of the Master's chair was presented by Charles Mathias, whilst the second banner from 1938 hangs on the left. Both were wisely framed in 1982 by George Bancroft during his occupancy of the Master's chair. They, too, with the latest Narberth Lodge banner that adorns the Master's place and was given by WBro Henry Thomas, bring a real distinction to the present room's east end.

After eight years at the De Rutzen Hotel negotiations had made available a ground floor building within the precinct of the Market Hall, just next door. This

Narberth Masonic Hall.

was also leased from the owner Baron De Rutzen though a year later the freehold was purchased for £36 7s 0d. To show further local continuity in the lodge here it is interesting to see that a descendant of the Baron, himself also bearing that title, was Wor Master in 1937, but was killed in action in Italy in 1944. By 1909 the premises, needing extension because of the rising membership, had a larger upstairs temple, a true winding stairway as in the 2° tracing board, and a useful assembly landing area. This sufficed until 1955 when the next door property was acquired with a view to extension but as this proved likely to be very costly another solution was looked for. The answer was the hall we have today.

In 1963 the Past Masters were informed that the local Wesleyan Chapel was coming up for sale and by 1964 they had purchased it. It was converted to its present use a year later and at 5.30pm on 15 October 1965 the temple dedication took place. The new temple was the old chapel interior with pulpit and pews removed but retaining the fine arched windows whilst the pillared canopy, the Master's and Wardens' pedestals and chairs, made by a Past Master in 1926, were able to be given a more ample setting. The vestry cum Sunday School became the dining room and an extension was built to provide essential other offices. In 1971 the neighbour's garden was bought so that by 1973 there was a decent kitchen for the wives who prepare the festive board, whilst in 1979 the new assembling room was added and of that a plaque near the entrance gives the story:

'This Assembly Room was erected and given to Narberth Lodge No 2001 by WBro C. H. Billings, PM Hainault Lodge No 4367 and Hon Member of Peace and Goodwill Lodge No 5801 (London) to commemorate the Happy Times spent in Pembrokeshire (1925-47) and in particular for the friendship of Members of 2001.'

Finally, in 1982, in preparation for the lodge's Centenary celebrations the whole building was redecorated, a new bench seating installed with blue vinyl cushioned seats and backs, the dais was extended allowing more room to the curved seating for Past Masters there, the red carpet surrounds to the chequered

Above left: *Narberth Hall with tracing boards displayed on central table.*

Above right: *The Master's position with bright morning star above the canopy.*

centre were renewed and other improvements made at a cost of £19,000 though of this some £8,000 was saved by voluntary work done by the members. In an address by Wor Bro Hugh Morgan of Narberth Lodge in the Kensington Lodge of Installed Masters most of the foregoing facts were provided and he closed his survey with these words: 'We feel confident that the brethren of the future will be grateful to us for providing them with a home worthy of their lodge.' As one looks round it today one cannot but be sensible of the truth of these words.

As has been said the most imposing item in the whole building is the canopied stall in which the Master takes his place. It stands out immediately as you enter the temple and it would be a feature that would grace any lodge room in which it was placed. The first items that draw the eye are two graceful pillars with oak shafts on square oak bases, each of the pillars having either an Ionic or Corinthian chapiter and above these, on a gilded base, a sphere delineating the terrestrial and celestrial globes. Above these pillars is a recessed oaken arch with a spiral decoration running round its centre and meeting at the apex first a wooden keystone with a gilt square and compasses, whilst above these is another box with a transparent five-pointed star on its front face. The rear of the recess is panelled in oak and this falls all the way to the ground behind with fluted panels around the lower half of the canopy. Hung over this rear wall is the latest Narberth banner showing another two pillars on a chequered pavement which has masonic emblems at its foot and a hart on a red and white garland at its upper edge. Above this creature is an all-seeing eye and the three Prince of Wales feathers with the motto 'Ich Dien'. Though the banner is in very modern style that compares interestingly with the other banners around it here brightly adorns this lovely item of furniture and contrasts also with the ancient black, carved ladder-back armchair that is used by the Master. The neat oak pedestal that stands before such a chair does not seem in the least to be out of place.

As we move west again we are bound to notice the solid chest in which the tracing boards are kept. It has often been remarked in these pages that brethren will do well to examine the boards of the lodges they visit and will be very surprised to see many differences between what at first they may imagine are standard works. This is certainly true for the 1° tracing board in this lodge and it may be of interest to note that the symbols found in this board in Pembrokeshire are exactly the same as those used in the Grand Temple in London. Those are not too frequent today and are all the more valuable for being preserved here.

As we take our leave of this freshly-used chapel, without its spire any longer but with extensions done in the most tasteful manner and using similar materials to those first employed, we are sure that those who must once have worshipped here will not now feel that its use is any less worthwhile. Here are taught a respect for God, a concern for neighbours and a right attendance to our own good conduct. It is an asset to the locality and a proper source of pride for the Narberth brethren who frequent it.

TENBY/Dinbych Y Pysgod

A few miles to the south lies the ancient seaside town of Tenby. The town was probably a Roman settlement, for many Roman coins have been found here. Beyond the harbour wall, where the fishermen's chapel of St Julian still stands, is Castle Hill. Little now remains of this castle though it was still standing in the 12th century but by the 15th Tenby was a prosperous little port and had walls that encircled the town and included five gates. It is close to and overshadowed by part of those walls that remain that we find the doorway to what is the somewhat undistinguished entrance of the Tenby Masonic Hall. The brother who might be among the many tourists that come to this sheltered resort, with its two beaches and glorious coastal scenery, may have to find a guide to steer him up the winding stair into the long low temple. He will pass a store room on his way.

We find that the Secretary of the Neyland Lodge was acting as a Provincial officer at the consecration of Tenby Lodge and one of their early initiates was that Charles Mathias, Esquire, whom we met as a founder of the Narberth Lodge. The Tenby Lodge members first met in the Assembly Rooms but this building's condition must have deteriorated for not only was a lodge committee set up in 1877 to look for new premises but in 1880 the Rooms were destroyed by fire. By then the lodge was housed in the present South Parade and arrangements had been made to let the masons have the additional storage room that is still in use. In 1877 the rent was raised to £10 with another rise to £14 in 1879 but at this point the brethren started serious talks with the 'Tenby Charity trustees to ensure that this property be a suitable place to meet more permanently'. Between £200 and £250 would be needed to effect this but the money must have been found because by 1880 there were plans for a formal dedication.

At this stage the lodge had the basic necessities of furniture when three valuable old tracing boards were presented by a brother who had 'found' them in Devonshire (though they are not extant today) and in 1883 Bro the Rev George Huntington, Rector of Tenby and Senior Warden, presented a very handsome oak chair for the Master's use. Sadly this was later found to be church property and now sits in St David's Cathedral. The banner then in use, though already beginning to suffer from constant wear, and especially when the brethren went in public procession to church or the laying of foundation stones, was a lovely example of the seamstress art and is now happily framed and preserved on the east wall of the lodge room. In 1909 the lady who repaired it was presented with Mr Law's book on 'The Church at Tenby' in appreciation of

Left: *The old Tenby Lodge Banner.*

Below left: *Wall Clock with masonic symbols on face.*

her labours as without her attentions it would probably not have survived. This standard was replaced by the present banner in 1930 at a cost of £45 and dedicated by the Grand Secretary of England, and though the same medallions with the town's arms are shown it has not had to stand the same wear and tear that affected its predecessor. Their preservation side by side certainly affirms the continuity of a lodge over a century and a quarter.

By 1911 the Trustees were leasing the hall to the lodge for 50 years at a yearly rent of £15 together with a piece of ground at the rear of the property. That lease would have ended in 1961 but by 1954 positive steps were taken to acquire the premises for the lodge and in November the members offered £1,750 for the freehold purchase price. The sale was agreed and in October 1959 the lodge added to its assets by acquiring still further land at the rear for the sum of £100. It is thus that the present premises became the sole possession and masonic hall of Tenby Lodge.

The echo of the Dunkirk evacuation comes in the minutes of June 1940 when the ante-room of the lodge was used as a club room for the large numbers of Belgian troops and civilians billeted in the town. The lodge had moreover meanwhile started a most useful library of books, and a set of inscribed gavels made from the old masonic temple in London before the present one was built to commemorate the sacrifice of brethren in the First World War. No one would pretend that the Tenby hall is exceptional but it has already had a long and happy history and perhaps the best memento of the time spent by so many on these premises is the very distinctive wall-clock that any visitor may be intrigued to see. With a dark blue face around which the minutes are marked by a circle of green markings there are also the hours indicated by 12 masonic symbols as follows:

1. a moon with a crescent face

2. a gavel. 2° ?

3. the square and compasses in 3° position

4. an equilateral triangle with an all-seeing eye at the centre

5. the pillar of J

6. a skull and cross bones — the 6th hour of the day

7. The pillar B

8. Triangle with plumb

9. 5 point star

10. trowel

11. a full-faced sun

12. a three-branched candlestick

One may not be in the hall at Tenby as long as in several of the others in this book but at least there are some items to remind us how special each hall can be to those whose home it will be.

Passing to the other end of the southern half of the Principality we come finally to Chepstow. Like Tenby and Narberth it has an historic past and the ruins of a castle that sustained several sieges during the Great Rebellion. Standing amongst steep cliffs at the junction of the Wye and Severn it has had a still more ancient history. The Britons knew it as 'Castell Gwent' (hence its current Welsh name of 'Cas-gwent') and the Saxons called it 'ciepestow' or 'Cheapstowe', 'the place where the merchants were' (to be compared with 'Cheapside' in London). Owing to the nature of the terrain hereabouts the Normans called it 'Steigwil' or 'The Castle at the Crook' for they heard the Welsh call the severe bend in the river 'Ystraigyl'. From the spellings of the place we have Estrighoel, Strigoielg, Strigoild, Striguille and Striguil. It will not be a surprise to learn that the original lodge and still the senior one in Chepstow is called 'Striguil Lodge No 2186'. There is now a Roderick Hill Lodge, No 8619, consecrated in 1975 but it will be with the history of the Striguil Lodge that we must naturally concern ourselves.

Freemasonry in Chepstow has also an established history. A letter from the Deputy Provincial Grand Master in Bristol on 23 July 1795 speaks of Chepstow brethren seeking to form a Lodge of Improvement so that, having prepared themselves with credit to discharge their duties (we would say, learn the ritual well enough) they might then consider forming a proper lodge. It would seem that they did so and eventually had a warrant in 1818. They then met in the George Inn but had several subsequent meeting places until they were erased in 1837 because there was a lack of regular members. Happily the original minute book of this lodge is one of the treasures of the new masonic hall here.

There is also a tradition, mentioned by Bro Thorp in his standard work on French Prisoners Lodges, that such a lodge met in this town but on making enquiries the evidence was apparently not available. All trace of it, if it existed, seems to have vanished. There was therefore a gap of 50 years in the town during which no mention of a lodge occurs. What is intriguing however is that when the Striguil Lodge comes to be consecrated in May 1887 there is already a masonic hall in Nelson Street with its own masonic emblem of the square and compasses on a squared panel of stone, which must have taken some time to prepare and which was so much used and suffering from wear and tear that by 1908 there had to be a search for another site. It is again very good that in the modern hall that exists today the visitor will see in the wall at the foot of the main staircase this very stone plaque which has the crossed square and compasses in the older position of the Fellow Craft.

The consecration even took place in this old hall and the usual 'seven (or more) masons to make it complete' was how the Striguil began. The author of this volume is very happy to note that the first Master was the WBro the Rev Daniel George Davies who also belonged to the Loyal Monmouth Lodge, and that within four years the lodge was parading in full regalia to St Mary's Church where, during the service, the Worshipful Master, assisted by his Wardens, 'unveiled the pulpit and presented it to the Vicar of Chepstow as a gift to the Church from the members of the Lodge'. (Striguil Centenary brochure.)

In the lodge itself a staff formerly belonging to an Abyssinian King was presented for use as a DC's wand and the very fine banner of the lodge was given in 1896. By 1901 there was the donation of a fine carved cedar wood collecting box which had been made by Boer prisoners who were under the charge of a lodge member when he was at St Helena. This is still used when a certain part of the First Degree is practised at the north east corner. It can thus be guessed that the lodge was settling down into a happy existence in the Nelson Street premises but time was beginning to tell on the structure and thus we learn that in 1908 a decision was taken to build a new masonic hall at Moor Street. It is a hall that still bears that date on a plaque for all to see. £200 would be raised in debentures and this would be added to the £100 already in hand.

In 1909 the landlords of their former premises wrote stating that as the keys of the Nelson Street hall had not been handed in they claimed another half year's rent and this was settled. The revelation that another company owned the earlier hall suggests that, as in Bangor, the name masonic hall was perhaps given to a property even when it was not occupied, even partly, by a lodge. It only increases the fascination of knowing why they so built such a hall when, or if, there was no Freemasonry in Chepstow, or whether they may have been intimations of renewed activity some time before 1887. Here is a subject for real local masonic research, starting with the archives of the local Cooperative Society.

Pictures of the Moor Street temple showing its interior arrangements reveal a place that must have received great care and attention and that possessed so much of what was able to be transferred to the eventual hall that the members enjoy today. The east was attractively panelled in black and white and the upholstered bench seats now appear. The old tracing boards are well displayed before the Junior Warden's pedestal and the two lovely fluted pillars with their perfect globes in frames at the head stood, as they still do, at the western end of the chequered flooring and before the Senior Warden's pedestal. In 1934 the Building Committee reported that the lease of these premises had been extended for 50 years at an annual rent of £10. To commemorate the lodge's Golden Jubilee in 1937 the bethren agreed to subscribe for a new Worshipful Master's chair and the pedestals for the three main officers. It is those that we see in use today.

It would have been quite natural for the lodge to expect to stay in such a pleasant and economic building for perpetuity. In 1952, however, the Worshipful Master, (later Sir) A. M. C. Jenour, stated that to purchase the building and to make the necessary extensions and provide more furniture for their growing numbers would cost £5,000 at least. It was thus decided that they would have to decline the offer to buy made by the hall's owners, Clarke's Estates. The next Provincial Grand Master of Monmouthshire, Col E. Roderick Hill, being a member of Striguil Lodge, it may well have been a disappointment to him not to see his mother lodge room develop. However he was to have the subsequent pleasure of seeing not only a much grander home for his brethren but to see it occupied by a lodge that bore his own name.

It was in 1970 that D. C. Powell gave details of a plot of land in Upper Nelson Street bordered on the far side by the Old School Hill. The cost of the site was £3,000 and as the Building Fund was at £1,560 an appeal for help had to be launched. The appeal was met with a swift response of support and the site was purchased. WBro Powell's plans were approved and a local building firm, Messrs James and White, were given the contract for the sum of £21,054. A limited company was formed under the chairmanship of WBro, A. I. Henderson and has remained in existence ever since. What made the whole process so very special was that as there was no money available for the many more furnishings that would be required in a vastly larger building some real self-help had to be engineered.

Under the supervision of WBro F. W. Griffith several groups of brethren got to work. About 100 second hand chairs were bought at an auction and the brethren paid £1.50 each for them. Each new owner then stripped, repaired and refurbished his chair before re-donating it to the Company for use in the dining

Masonic temple at Chepstow with pillars in the west.

room. About 100 cinema seats were discovered in a locally disused cinema and these were obtained free of charge. They were taken apart, degreased, completely stripped, repolished and re-upholstered. The older existing bench seats were given the same treatment. In all some 1,075 hours of work on the seats were provided. When one looks at the remarkable result of all this labour — the interior decoration, the new heating installation and electrical wiring, and the large oak bar, not to mention the platforms for the seating, the steel fire escape, the massive and striking 'G' and the donated Wilton carpet, one cannot but be deeply impressed by the sheer dedication and affection thus showered upon the only new purpose-built temple to be erected in Monmouthshire since the last such hall was commenced in Tredegar in 1904. Anyone who hears the tones of the beautiful electronic organ, sits down to cutlery and crockery at dinner or admires the trees and shrubs around the 15 steps leading in stages of three, five and seven to the main entrance, is savouring the sheer hard work of countless hours put in by many whose names may never be mentioned but whose efforts have now made Freemasonry here a delightful experience. Even as you walk through the pair of fine panelled doors under an automatically activated outside light you are being reminded of the service of one in particular who represented the lodge during these very important days. He was C. L. Singleton, PAGDC, who for 32 years was a devoted Secretary of the lodge and who played an immense part in organising the whole transfer to this new centre.

Just as the older premises in Moor Street still carry their masonic panel of '19 ✠ 08' so this large new rectangular hall, so prominently situated on the main road round the town, also bears its own sign to show to the town another stage in its masonic growth. Here the brethren can learn how to communicate the beneficial effects of the Craft to the community at large and strive to transmit, from generation to generation, the same inspiration that led those brethren of 200 years ago to strive to so perform their 'duties' that they might eventually have what there now is — a modern hall for Striguil and Roderick Hill that anyone can be proud of.

INDEX

People and Places

Objects and Symbols